# GUY STUFF
### *in the*
# SCRIPTURES

## OTHER BOOKS BY MIKE WINDER

*Presidents and Prophets:*
*The Story of America's Presidents and the LDS Church*

*Life Lessons from Fathers of Faith:*
*Inspiring True Stories About Latter-day Dads*
(with coauthor Gary W. Toyn)

*When the White House Comes to Zion*
(with coauthor Ronald L. Fox)

*Called to Serve: Celebrating Missionary Work around the World*

# GUY STUFF

## in the

# SCRIPTURES

## Mike Winder

Covenant Communications, Inc.

Published by Covenant Communications, Inc.
American Fork, Utah

Printed in the United States of America
First Printing: April 2014

22 21 20 19 18 17 16 15 14      10 9 8 7 6 5 4 3 2 1

ISBN 978-1-62108-753-3

To my dear wife, Karyn, who has helped this guy be the man I am and who has been so amazingly supportive of this and so many other projects in my life.

And to the guys closest to me,
who are all my heroes in their own ways:
Michael Winder & John Winder (sons)
Kent Winder (dad) & Rob Hermansen (father-in-law)
Nate Winder & Isaac Winder (brothers)
Matt Newton & Tom Larsen (brothers-in-law)
Don Pratt, Robert Hermansen, Layne Beacham
& Steve Hermansen (brothers-in-law)
Travis Hathcock & Caleb Hathcock (step-brothers)
Cecil Jepson (grandpa)

## ACKNOWLEDGMENTS

I appreciate the support and partnership of the team at Covenant Communications for making this fun book a reality. Barry Evans, Kathy Gordon, Robby Nichols, Ron Brough and the rest of the crew shared their expertise and enthusiasm to help launch this project. I am especially indebted to Samantha Millburn, my amazing editor, who continuously polished and improved this book with her skills and suggestions. Margaret Weber-Longoria and her design team turned mere words into the magic of a book with their layout, especially Christina Marcano, who did a terrific job as the designer of this book.

Numerous friends sent in "favorite funny verses," which I appreciate. Years of listening to parents, family, seminary teachers, institute instructors, and Sunday school teachers provided a foundation of gospel knowledge that helped shape this book. I especially appreciate Jayme Asbell-Luckau, who provided several custom illustrations uniquely for this book.

The great things about this book I attribute to God and the many others named and unnamed here. The crazy ideas, lousy attempts at humor, and any mistakes are my own!

Mike Winder

# CONTENTS

# WHY GUY STUFF IN THE SCRIPTURES?
## —— INTRODUCTION ——

The scriptures are wonderful things. By studying the scriptures, we can find answers to life's questions, bring the Spirit into our lives and homes, and better prepare to return to our Father in Heaven. All of us can improve our lives by reading the scriptures more, pondering their messages, and understanding what they are trying to teach us. President Howard W. Hunter taught, "This is the most profitable of all study in which we could engage."[1]

As priesthood holders and prospective priesthood holders, men have an added duty to immerse themselves in the word of God. The Lord has said, "Wherefore, now let every man learn his duty, and to act in the office in which he is appointed, in all diligence" (D&C 107:99). As husbands and fathers, we can be better men if we are more familiar with the holy scriptures and more fluent in the words of God.

As we find new ways to look at the scriptures—including fun ways—we will become more familiar with them, less intimidated by them, and naturally drawn to their pages again and again. Wading through the standard works should not be just a chore;

1 Howard W. Hunter, "Reading the Scriptures," *Ensign*, Nov. 1979, 64.

it can become a joy! President Gordon B. Hinckley said, "I hope that for you this will become something far more enjoyable than a duty; that, rather, it will become a love affair with the word of God."[2]

You may have read the Book of Mormon ten times and be a seminary graduate, but you still have the obligation to repeatedly rediscover the scriptures to find new meanings for your ever-changing life. President Spencer W. Kimball said, "I am convinced that each of us, at least some time in our lives, must discover the scriptures for ourselves—and not just discover them once, but rediscover them again and again."[3]

The point of this book is to encourage you to rediscover the scriptures by looking at them anew through a variety of perspectives. In this book, we will look at everything from boats and weapons to heroes and villains, food and fortune to humor and science. So, please, have fun with this book! Have fun with the scriptures! There are hundreds of verses referenced in these pages, and hopefully, this will be merely a jumping-off point for you to immerse yourself in your own adventure in the scriptures.

I have loved the scriptures since childhood. I learned to read as I followed along in the Church's *Scripture Stories for Beginning Readers* and listened to the accompanying cassette tapes. When I was in Primary, the prophet at the time, Spencer W. Kimball, inspired me with his story of when he was

2 Gordon B. Hinckley, "The Light within You," *Ensign*, May 1995, 99.
3 Spencer W. Kimball, "How Rare a Possession—the Scriptures!" *Ensign*, Sept. 1976, 4.

a boy himself and accomplished a goal of reading the Bible cover to cover.[4] This motivated me, and as a seven-year-old, I began reading the Old Testament. It took me years, but I was pleased to finish all four standard works before I turned twelve. The scriptures have been an important part of my life ever since. The words in those books are true, and I testify that they are God's instructions to us and that our lives are better when we are immersed in their pages. May this book inspire you to dive into the scriptures and to increase your love for them.

---

4 Pres. Kimball's story is referenced many times, most recently in Garrett H. Garff, "Spencer W. Kimball: Man of Action" *Ensign*, Jan. 2007, 63.

# One
# GADGETS, TOOLS, AND CONSTRUCTION

Guys keep the Home Depot in business. They tend to have an innate desire to build things, fix things, and putter with things. For good or for bad, in the workforce, 93 percent of construction workers, 94 percent of mechanical engineers, and 98 percent of carpenters are men.[5] So when men see gadgets and gizmos, tools, and construction projects in the scriptures, they get excited, which then makes them wonder . . . .

## WHAT DID NEPHI KNOW ABOUT MAKING TOOLS?

Nephi not only knew about steel, but he also knew enough about metallurgy to identify Laban's blade as "most precious steel" (1 Nephi 4:9). After all, when the Lord tells Nephi to build a ship, his first question is, "Whither shall I go that I may find ore to molten, that I may make tools . . . ?" (1 Nephi 17:9). Just give me the ore, he says, and I know how to make tools. The man was a handy metallurgist and toolmaker. Later, Nephi was thrilled to find various ores in the promised land because he knew what he could make out of them. "And I did teach my people to build buildings, and to work in all manner of wood, and of iron, and of copper, and of brass, and of steel, and of gold, and of silver, and of precious ores, which were in great abundance" (2 Nephi 5:15).

And once Nephi made the tools, he was very skilled in using them. "And I, Nephi, did build a temple; and I did construct it after the manner of the temple of Solomon save it were not built of so many precious things. . . . But . . . the workmanship thereof was

5 Bureau of Labor Statistics, U.S. Department of Labor, 2012.

exceedingly fine." And Nephi encouraged his people to build things too. "And it came to pass that I, Nephi, did cause my people to be industrious, and to labor with their hands" (2 Nephi 5:16–17).

## WHERE ELSE ARE TOOLS MENTIONED IN THE SCRIPTURES?

Tools are mentioned in the Old Testament but are viewed as a necessary evil and are considered rather unclean. It didn't help that tools were used to shape idols, like the "graving tool" Aaron used to fashion "a molten calf" (Exodus 32:4). In fact, the Lord stated, "If thou wilt make me an altar of stone, thou shalt not build it of hewn stone: for if thou lift up thy tool upon it, thou hast polluted it" (Exodus 20:25). He also said regarding tools around the sacred altars, "Thou shalt not lift up any iron tool upon them" (Deuteronomy 27:5). Even when the temple was being built, the Lord didn't want tools anywhere nearby. "And the house, when it was in building, was built of stone made ready before it was brought thither: so that there was neither hammer nor axe nor any tool of iron heard in the house, while it was in building" (1 Kings 6:7).

Not helping the reputation of tools in the Old Testament, Jael used a hammer and nail to kill Sisera. She "took a nail of the tent, and took an hammer in her hand, and went softly unto him, and smote the nail into his temples, and fastened it into the ground: for he was fast asleep and weary. So he died" (Judges 4:21).

On the other hand, in the New Testament, tools play a vital role in the livelihood of the holy family and in the death of the Savior. We learn that Mary's husband,

Joseph, was a carpenter (see Matthew 13:55) and that Jesus himself learned the trade. It was asked about Jesus, "Is not this the carpenter, the son of Mary . . . ?" (Mark 6:3). The early Christian writer Justin Martyr (d. 165) wrote that Jesus's woodworking specialized in yokes and ploughs.[6] Later, of course, nails were pounded into the Savior's hands, wrists, and feet as He died for us on the cross at Golgotha.

## WHEN WERE CHARIOTS FIRST USED IN THE SCRIPTURES?

Chariots are mentioned 162 times in the scriptures and were a primary means of getting around for the wealthy and the military. Just as guys today love their cars, guys in scriptural times loved their chariots. The first chariots date back to 2000 B.C. in modern-day Kazakhstan. They spread from there until they reached Egypt a few hundred years later. When Joseph was sold into Egypt in about 1700 B.C., we see the first Biblical mention of chariots: "And he made him to ride in the second chariot which he had" (Genesis 41:43). These would have been very new to Egypt at the time, as there is no archeological evidence of chariots in Egypt before then, but they stuck in the culture, and around 1500 B.C., the Egyptians developed a yoke saddle for the horses pulling the chariots, giving the charioteers of Egypt's army a speed, strength, and mobility that could not be matched by any infantry of the age.

The chariot became an even more integral part of Egypt's military by the time Moses led the Israelites out of Egypt and across the Red Sea on dry land in 1476 B.C. Their chariot had a cross-bar wheel construction, which enabled the speed needed for military success. They also had a large shield in front and were a

---

6 David A. Fiensy, *Jesus the Galilean: Soundings in a First Century Life*, (New Jersey: Gorgias Press LLC, 2007), 68–69.

much more stable **GREATEST CHARIOT BATTLE EVER! IN** platform for archers **PERHAPS THE GREATEST CHARIOT BATTLE** than traditional **EVER, THE BATTLE OF KADESH IN 1274 B.C.,** horseback. With **RAMSES II LED THE EGYPTIANS IN A CONFLICT** this state-of-the-art **INVOLVING 5,000–6,000 CHARIOTS. THIS** vehicle, Pharaoh and **IS MANY MORE THAN PURSUED MOSES AND** "six hundred chosen **THE ISRAELITES.** chariots, and all the chariots of Egypt" (Exodus 14:7) pursued the children of Israel as they fled, but the waters of the Red Sea still "covered the chariots, and the horsemen, and all the host of Pharaoh that came into the sea" (Exodus 14:28).

## WHY WERE THERE TWO SPINDLES ON THE LIAHONA?

"And within the ball were two spindles," Nephi explained. "And the one pointed the way whither we should go into the wilderness" (1 Nephi 16:10). Alma taught how the Liahona worked: "Therefore, if they had faith to believe that God could cause that those spindles should point the way they should go, behold, it was done; therefore they had this miracle" (Alma 37:40). Having two pointers, or spindles, could have meant that when the spindles lined up, they were pointing in the right direction. Robert L. Bunker, a chief engineer at the Jet Propulsion Laboratory in Pasadena, California, said, "To appreciate the elegance of the Liahona's design, from an engineer's viewpoint, is to understand the function of the *second* pointer. Since a single pointer is always pointing a direction, it was likely the role of the second pointer to provide the necessary additional information about whether the Liahona was 'operational,' meaning that the pointing information from the first pointer was reliable." He also said, "This proposed purpose for the second pointer conforms to a well-established engineering principle used in modern fault-tolerant computer systems called 'voting,' in which two identical process states are compared and declared *correct* if they are the same, and *incorrect* if they are different."[7]

---

7 Robert L. Bunker, "The Design of the Liahona and the Purpose of the Second Spindle," *Journal of Book of Mormon Studies* 3, no. 2, (Provo, Utah: Maxwell Institute, 1994): 6, 1.

## COULD THE LIAHONA "TEXT MESSAGE"?

Once, when Lehi's party was arguing about where to find food, he was told, "Look upon the ball, and behold the things which are written" (1 Nephi 16:26). So in addition to the spindles providing direction, writing also miraculously appeared on the ball. As if the otherworldly assembly of the Liahona wasn't strange enough, the writing really freaked everybody out. "And it came to pass that when my father beheld the things which were written upon the ball, he did fear and tremble exceedingly, and also my brethren and the sons of Ishmael and our wives." Nephi tells us that not only were there words appearing on the ball but that they would also change. "And there was also written upon them a new writing, which was plain to be read, which did give us understanding concerning the ways of the Lord; and it was written and changed from time to time, according to the faith and diligence which we gave unto it" (1 Nephi 16:27, 29). It probably didn't give time and temperature like a bank's electronic marquee, but the text that appeared gave Lehi's family additional guidance as they followed the "ball of curious workmanship" to the New World.

## WHAT WAS THE FATE OF THE LIAHONA?

This sacred compass became a kingly relic of sorts and was passed down with the sword of Laban and the brass plates. For example, King Benjamin handed them all off to Mosiah I in Mosiah 1:16. Alma explains that these things were saved for a reason: "And it may suffice if I only say they are preserved for a wise purpose, which purpose is known unto God" (Alma 37:12). Around 1 B.C., we see Nephi, son of Helaman, depart from the land of Zarahemla and pass down to his son the plates of Nephi and the brass plates—but the Liahona is no longer listed (see 3 Nephi 1:2). Maybe it is because the sacred compass had another mission to fulfill, maybe aiding Nephi as he journeyed away from Zarahemla, or it was inadvertently omitted from the record. In 1823, when Joseph Smith catalogued the items in the stone box in the Hill Cumorah, he listed three things—"the plates, the Urim and Thummim, and the breastplate"—but no Liahona (Joseph Smith—History 1:52). We do know that in 1829 Joseph Smith and the Three Witnesses to the Book of Mormon were also shown through angelic means "the miraculous directors which were given to Lehi while in the wilderness" (D&C 17:1).

## HOW MANY URIM AND THUMMIM WERE THERE?

A Urim and Thummim is a unique device that allows a person to receive revelation from God. There seem to be two, maybe three sets in existence. The first one to appear was recorded in about

2200 B.C., during the lifetime of the brother of Jared. He was given a Urim and Thummim "upon the mount, when he talked with the Lord face to face" (D&C 17:1). It is appropriate that this prophet, who was present when the languages diverged at the Tower of Babel, now possessed the gadget designed "for the purpose of interpreting languages" (Mosiah 28:14). This set was passed down through the Jaredite seers of old until Mosiah II received them. It was then handed down to Alma, Helaman, and eventually Moroni, who hid the Urim and Thummim in the Hill Cumorah so Joseph Smith could find them in the latter days and use them to help translate the gold plates.

A second Urim and Thummim appeared in about 2100 B.C.: "And I, Abraham, had the Urim and Thummim, which the Lord my God had given unto me, in Ur of the Chaldees" (Abraham 3:1). Abraham used these to receive instructions about the cosmos and God's home near Kolob.

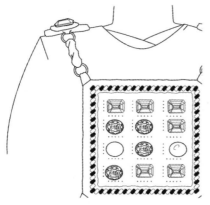

Moses was asked to craft a breastplate as he was building the tabernacle and outfitting the priests in about 1450 B.C. He was then instructed, "And thou shalt put in the breastplate of judgment the Urim and the Thummim; and they shall be upon Aaron's heart, when he goeth in before the Lord" (Exodus 28:30). We don't know if those precious seer stones, the Urim and Thummim, were passed down through the patriarchs from Abraham to Moses over 600 years or if this was a new one. They are mentioned again in the days of King Saul, in about 1050 B.C. (see 1 Samuel 28:6) but are noted as lost once the Jews returned to Jerusalem from Babylon in about 538 B.C. (see Ezra 2:63). They may have disappeared during the Babylonian captivity when the invaders "took all the holy vessels of the Lord, both great and small, and the ark of God, and the king's treasures, and carried them away into Babylon" (Apocrypha, 1 Esdras 1:54).

In the future, the righteous inheritors of the celestial kingdom will each receive their own Urim and Thummim, and "this earth, in its sanctified and immortal state, will be made like unto crystal and will be a Urim and Thummim" (D&C 130:8–11).

## WHICH IS "URIM," AND WHICH IS "THUMMIM," AND WHY IS THE SET PLURAL?

Translated literally from Hebrew, *urim* means "lights" and *thummim* means "wholeness," but taken allegorically, *urim and thummim*, according to scholars' interpretation means "lights and perfections," "revelation and truth," or "doctrine and truth." Joseph Smith taught that they were "two transparent stones set in the rim of a bow fastened to a breast plate."[8] Indeed, it seems that *urim* brought light, revelation, and illumination but was not a whole, complete, or perfect view without *thummim*.

---

8 *HC*, 4:537.

The Urim and Thummim were often placed in bows fastened to a breastplate, likely for ease of use. Like spectacles of sorts, it seems that by looking through the transparent stones of Urim and Thummim, one could translate languages and receive revelations.

As Hebrew words ending in the suffix -im, urim and thummim are plural words. This could be because they contain (or, more accurately, reveal) lights and truths. However, some Jewish scholars believe this is actually a case of pluralis intensivus—a unique outlier in the Hebrew language where special singular words are pluralized to enhance their sacredness or majesty.[9]

**THUMMIM AND URIM?** THE URIM AND THUMMIM ARE ALWAYS MENTIONED WITH URIM FIRST, WITH ONE EXCEPTION. IN DEUTERONOMY 33:8, WE READ: "AND OF LEVI HE SAID, LET THY THUMMIM AND THY URIM BE WITH THY HOLY ONE." IN 1 SAMUEL 28:6, WE LEARN THREE WAYS GOD REVEALED ANSWERS IN THE OLD TESTAMENT, AND THUMMIM IS LEFT OUT (PROBABLY JUST AS AN ABBREVIATION): "AND WHEN SAUL INQUIRED OF THE LORD, THE LORD ANSWERED HIM NOT, NEITHER BY DREAMS, NOR BY URIM, NOR BY PROPHETS."

## WHAT SIMPLE MACHINE APPEARS IN THE PEARL OF GREAT PRICE?

Scientists in the Renaissance classified six simple machines that provided mechanical advantage: the lever, wheel and axle, pulley, inclined plane, wedge, and screw. In Joseph Smith—History, Joseph uses a lever. He described arriving at the Hill Cumorah and finding what Moroni had hid for him: "On the west side of this hill, not far from the top, under a stone of considerable size, lay the plates, deposited in a stone box." Joseph then described the stone of considerable size: "This stone was thick and rounding in the middle on the upper side, and thinner towards the edges, so that the middle part of it was visible above the ground, but the edge all around was covered with earth" (JS—H 1:51).

---

9 "Urim and Thummim," *Jewish Encyclopedia*, accessed January 27, 2014, http://www.jewishencyclopedia.com/articles/14609-urim-and-thummim.

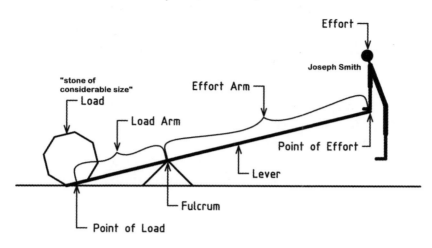

So how was he to remove the stone when he was young and by himself?

With a simple machine!

"Having removed the earth, I obtained a lever, which I got fixed under the edge of the stone, and with a little exertion raised it up" (JS—H 1:52). Joseph's lever worked, as all levers do, by pivoting a rigid beam (probably a large stick) on a fulcrum (a smaller rock, perhaps, or maybe just the edge of the ground). Joseph's input force resulted in a greater output force than he could have produced otherwise, resulting in leverage.

The mathematical principle of levers states that the longer the beam from the fulcrum, assuming the beam does not bend or break, the greater the leverage magnifies the initial input. Archimedes illustrated this principle by saying, "Give me a place to stand, and I will move the earth."[10] In Joseph's case, he needed only a place to stand, and with his lever, he removed the considerable stone and uncovered the box of Book of Mormon treasures.

---

10 Alan L. Mackay, *A Dictionary of Scientific Quotations* (London: Institute of Physics Publishing, 1991), 11.

## WHICH WAS A LARGER CONSTRUCTION PROJECT, SOLOMON'S PALACE OR SOLOMON'S TEMPLE?

During his forty-year reign in the tenth century B.C., Solomon reached the zenith of Israel's wealth and power and translated much of that into major construction projects. He constructed means of supplying Jerusalem with fresh water, secured the city's defenses, rebuilt other cities, erected military outposts, and founded the port city of Ezion-Geber on the shores of the Red Sea's Gulf of Aqaba. But his most famous projects were the temple and his palace.

Solomon brought in Hiram of Tyre as the master architect for these massive and special projects. "[Hiram] was a widow's son of the tribe of Naphtali, and his father was a man of Tyre, a worker in brass: and he was filled with wisdom, and understanding, and cunning to work all works in brass. And he came to king Solomon, and wrought all his work" (1 Kings 7:14).

Solomon's temple was built over a seven-year period on Mount Zion, now called the Temple Mount. It was patterned after the Tabernacle of Moses, with the dimensions of the building being exactly twice the size. There were elaborate walls and courtyards, but the temple building itself was 60 cubits long (90 feet), 20 cubits broad (30 feet), and 30 cubits high (45 feet). There was also a porch in front that was 10 cubits deep (15 feet) (see 1 Kings 6:2–3). This

elaborate construction project also included pillars, a molten font, detailed carvings, and walls, floors, and ceilings lined with gold.

Aside from constructing the temple, for thirteen years, Solomon had laborers building a royal palace on Ophel, a hilly promontory in central Jerusalem. This mansion was enormous, with a campus of several interconnected structures. The House of the Forest of Lebanon was one part: "The length thereof was an hundred cubits [150 feet], and the breadth thereof fifty cubits [75 feet], and the height thereof thirty cubits [45 feet]" (1 Kings 7:2). The Hall of Pillars was another: "The length thereof was fifty cubits [75 feet], and the breadth thereof thirty cubits [45 feet]" (1 Kings 7:6). Then he had a throne room, or "porch of judgment," as well as a house specifically for Pharaoh's daughter. This palace complex had elaborate woodwork from the cedars of Lebanon, ornate carvings, and gold throughout.

Though by modern standards both structures are not enormous, they were considered large for their day. The famous temple of Solomon, the focal point of the faith, the resting place of the ark of the covenant, and the legendary house of the Lord had a floor space of 2,700 square feet. The house of Solomon, which took almost twice as long to construct, was exponentially larger than the temple. It had a square footage of at least 18,625 square feet—11,250 square feet for the House of the Forest of Lebanon, 3,375 square feet for the Hall of Pillars, and at least 2,000 square feet for the throne room and the house of Pharaoh's daughter. This puts the temple of Solomon in perspective as more of a king's chapel, with his nine-times-larger palace close by. This also underscores some of Solomon's pride issues that brought about his downfall in the end, when he put the idols of his wives ahead of the one true God.

## WAS WICKED KING HEROD REALLY "THE GREATEST BUILDER IN JEWISH HISTORY"?

King Herod—yes, the tyrant of the Christmas story—has been called "the greatest builder in Jewish history," and accurately so.[11] He employed 1,000 priests as masons and carpenters to rebuild the temple in Jerusalem in a year and a half and greatly enlarged it while he was at it. This was part of his effort to win favor with his subjects, who never did like him. As part of his attempt to curry favor with the Jews, Herod also built

11 Ken Spiro, "History Crash Course #31: Herod the Great," aish.com, accessed January 27, 2014, http://www.aish.com/jl/h/cc/48942446.html.

large stone enclosures to protect the Cave of the Patriarchs (burial place of Abraham and Sarah, Isaac and Rebecca, and Jacob and Leah), and Abraham's well at Mamre in Hebron. Herod built a town and harbor on the Mediterranean Sea called Caesarea Maritima, and he built the legendary mountaintop fortress Masada. Atop the highest peak in the Judean desert, he built Herodium, a small town, palace, and fortress. He also constructed aqueducts and facilities to improve the water supply to Jerusalem.

But when you think about it, wicked kings often were excessive builders. King Noah is the Book of Mormon example: "And it came to pass that king Noah built many elegant and spacious buildings. . . . And he also built him a spacious palace. . . . And it came to pass that he built a tower near the temple; yea, a very high tower." His appetite for building was insatiable. "And it came to pass that he caused many buildings to be built in the land Shilom; and he caused a great tower to be built on the hill north of the land Shilom. . . . And it came to pass that he planted vineyards round about in the land; and he built wine-presses" (Mosiah 11:8–15).

## HOW EFFECTIVE WERE CAPTAIN MORONI'S FORTIFICATIONS?

When the Nephites' enemies ran into the Nephites' new fortifications, they were blown away: "And it came to pass that the Lamanites, or the Amalickiahites, were exceedingly astonished at their manner of preparation for war." These fortifications were built "in a manner which never had been known among the children of Lehi" (Alma 49:8–9).

First, Lamanites were met with what military historians call a "glacis"— an embankment that sloped up toward the protective walls: "Moroni had stationed an army by the borders of the city, and they had cast up dirt round about to shield them from the arrows and the stones of the Lamanites" (Alma 49:2).

Second, the Nephites' opponents were met with a moat, for Captain Moroni instructed his team to "commence in digging up heaps

of earth round about all the cities" (Alma 50:1). This meant that the only way in or out of these fortifications was through a secure gateway over the heavily defended moat—"Neither could they come upon them save it was by their place of entrance" (Alma 49:4).

Next, the fortifications included walls of "timbers, yea, works of timbers built up to the height of a man, round about the cities." Moroni "caused that upon those works of timbers there should be a frame of pickets built upon the timbers round about; and they were strong and high" (Alma 50:2–3).

To further protect the areas along the walls, Moroni "caused towers to be erected that overlooked those works of pickets, and he caused places of security to be built upon those towers, that the stones and the arrows of the Lamanites could not hurt them." This gave the Nephites the strategic higher ground against any approaching army. "And they were prepared that they could cast stones from the top thereof, according to their pleasure and their strength, and slay him who should attempt to approach near the walls of the city" (Alma 50:4–5).

So, did the fortifications work? The scriptures say, "Now at this time the chief captains of the Lamanites were astonished exceedingly, because of the wisdom of the Nephites in preparing their places of security." In fact, the Lamanites were devastated: "Behold, how great was their disappointment" (Alma 49:4–5). The fortifications of the Nephite cities worked so well that they marked the turning point in the war.

Researcher Chris Alvarez points out that the battles before the fortification efforts were bloody losses for the Nephites: "Had battles like this been allowed to continue, the Nephite population would have been wiped out by the end of the war," he said. "The Lamanites would undoubtedly have survived because they were far more numerous than the Nephites."[12] But the defensive advantage Moroni created made the difference. Historian-General Mormon was so impressed with Captain Moroni that he named his son after him and spent considerable hand-etched pages of gold describing Captain Moroni's military genius and triumphs.

## HOW TALL WAS THE TOWER OF BABEL ANYWAY?

Around 2200 B.C., people on the plains of Shinar said, "Go to, let us build us a city and a tower, whose top may reach unto heaven" (Genesis 11:4). This was the origin of Babel (later known as Babylon) and the infamous Tower of Babel. So how tall was this ancient skyscraper? Genesis does not say, and the book of Ether in the Book of Mormon simply calls it "the great tower," without any quantification of its height (Ether 1:33). The Jewish-Roman historian Flavius Josephus wrote of the tower: "It grew very high, sooner than any one could expect; but the thickness of it was so great, and it was so strongly built, that thereby its great height seemed, upon the view, to be less than it really was."[13]

But how high was it? Some archaeologists wonder if the Great Ziggurat of Babylon, built in that time period, is actually the Tower of Babel spoken of in the scriptures. It was 300 feet tall and was destroyed by Alexander the Great. Gregory of Tours, a Roman historian and early Christian bishop, also claimed that the Tower of

---

12 Chris Alvarez, "Captain Moroni's Stratagem: Straight from the Scriptures," *Selections from the Religious Education Student Symposium 2008* (Provo, UT: Religious Studies Center, Brigham Young University, 2008), 99.
13 Flavius Josephus, *Antiquities of the Jews*, 1.4.3.

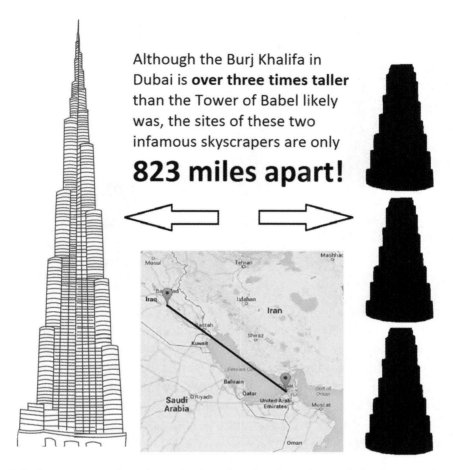

Although the Burj Khalifa in Dubai is **over three times taller** than the Tower of Babel likely was, the sites of these two infamous skyscrapers are only **823 miles apart!**

Babel was 200 cubits (300 feet) in height. But this isn't high enough to fit the descriptions of a "tower reaching to the clouds" or seemingly being the highest man-made object of the ancient world. After all, the Great Pyramid of Giza in Egypt, well known in the ancient world and completed in 2540 B.C., was 481 feet high.

Other claims of the height of the Tower of Babel are ridiculously high. One writing says "its height amounted to 5433 cubits and 2 palms" (book of Jubilees 10:20–21). This puts the structure at 8,150 feet—more than a mile and a half tall. The English Marco Polo, world traveler John Mandeville, reported in the 1350s that the locals in Babylon claimed the Tower of Babel was 64 furlongs

The Tower of Babel would look enormous in ancient Babylon or even modern Salt Lake City.

Eiffel Tower - 1063 feet    Tower of Babel    Space Needle    Church Office Building    Statue of Liberty
                            695 feet          605 feet        420 feet                 305 feet

(about 8 miles) high. An especially wild claim was that of Giovanni Villani, the Italian diplomat and historian who wrote in the year 1300 that the tower was 4,000 paces high (232,000 feet). That would put the towers height at 44 miles into space. British scientist J. E. Gordon calculated that a brick or stone structure higher than 1.3 miles would exceed the crushing strength of the materials and collapse under its own weight.[14]

**TODAY'S TALLEST BUILDINGS** THE TALLEST STRUCTURE IN THE WORLD TODAY IS THE BURJ KHALIFA IN DUBAI, UNITED ARAB EMIRATES. IT HAS 163 FLOORS AND A HEIGHT OF 2,722 FEET. THE KINGDOM TOWER IN JEDDAH, SAUDI ARABIA, IS UNDER CONSTRUCTION AND, WHEN COMPLETED IN 2019, WILL SURPASS THE BURJ KHALIFA AT AN AMAZING 3,281 FEET—EXACTLY ONE FOOT MORE THAN ONE KILOMETER. IT WAS ORIGINALLY SLATED TO BE A MILE HIGH, BUT THE SOILS REPORT RULED OUT THAT MUCH CONCENTRATED WEIGHT, SO THE BUILDERS ARE SHOOTING TO CONSTRUCT THE FIRST BUILDING TO EXCEED A KILOMETER INSTEAD. IRONICALLY, BOTH OF THESE SUPER SKYSCRAPERS ARE WITHIN A FEW HUNDRED MILES OF THE TOWER OF BABEL SITE.

---

14 J. E. Gordon, *Structures: or Why Things Don't Fall Down* (Cambridge, MA: De Capo Press, 1981).

So what is a reasonable height for the Tower of Babel? One apocryphal source claims the "tower of strife" was a "height of four hundred and sixty-three cubits" (3 Baruch 3:7). This would put the Tower of Babel at an impressive—but not unreasonable—695 feet. It would make it the tallest man-made structure in history until the Eiffel Tower was erected in Paris in 1889, its height reaching 1,063 feet to set the new record. We may never know in this life how tall the tower was, but the height in Baruch seems most likely. And remember, "thus saith the Lord unto you concerning the Apocrypha—There are many things contained therein that are true, and it is mostly translated correctly" (D&C 91:1).

# Two

# BEAUTIES OF THE BIBLE

Women have been an essential part of a guy's life since the days when Adam followed Eve right out of the Garden of Eden, and the scriptures highlight some powerful women. Who would have been the best catch? We can use scriptural clues to piece together our rankings. See if you agree! No salty women here (sorry, Lot!).

**10. DELILAH**—Loved by the strong Samson, Delilah had such influence over him that he revealed the secret of his strength (his long hair) to her to prove that he loved her. Bad idea. This gal betrayed him and had his head shaved while he slept in her lap, leading to Samson's downfall. Clearly a beauty, so she makes our list, but she was not a very nice one, so we relegate Delilah to the last of our top ten. (See Judges 16)

**9. TABITHA**—Tabitha's Aramaic name means "gazelle," and although her name in Greek was rather funny (Dorcas), this lady of Joppa did great things. The New Testament says, "This woman was full of good works and almsdeeds which she did" (Acts 9:36). When she became ill and died, all the widows cried and showed Peter the many coats and clothes she had made for them through the years. Who could not love such a saint? Because so many deeply loved Tabitha, Peter raised her from the dead. Go, Tabitha!

**8. LEAH**—Described in Genesis 29:17 as "tender eyed," but not gorgeous like her younger sister Rachel, Leah makes a strong case for herself; however, there has been great debate on what this "tender eyed" comment means. The New American Bible translates the

line as, "Leah had lovely eyes." Some scholars think a Hebrew with "tender eyes" had eyes that were blue or light in color. But the New International Version translates it as, "Leah had weak, or delicate, eyes." Maybe saying Leah was tender eyed had nothing to do with her eyes at all and was just a figure of speech. Some Bible scholars think saying someone was "tender eyed" may just have been a polite way of saying she was not very pretty.[15]

T h i s is like saying that a BYU coed has a "sweet spirit." But maybe it was a sincere compliment, and in ancient Israel, it could have been like us saying a beautiful woman is "easy on the eyes." There's potential here for Jacob's first wife, but uncertainty too, so we place her at number eight on our list. (See Genesis 29)

**BEWARE THE ANGRY WOMAN!**
"IT IS BETTER TO DWELL IN THE WILDERNESS, THAN WITH A CONTENTIOUS AND AN ANGRY WOMAN."
PROVERB 21:19

**7. BATHSHEBA**—Well known throughout antiquity for her attractiveness, Bathsheba brought down a king with her looks! David, while walking along the roof one evening, saw this lovely neighbor washing herself, "and the woman was

---

15 For various translations of this verse, see "Genesis 29:17," Biblehub, accessed January 27, 2014, http://biblehub.com/genesis/29–17.htm.

very beautiful to look upon" (2 Samuel 11:2). Unfortunately, he committed adultery with her, she became pregnant, and he sent her husband, Uriah, to the front of the battle, where he was killed. That lustful sin haunted David the remainder of his life, and though he worked with the prophet Nathan to repent, his reign was never what it could have been. As for Bathsheba, she also worked with the prophet Nathan and appears to have repented (see 1 Kings 1), become the mother of Solomon, and arrived at number seven on our list.

**6. REBEKAH**—When Isaac was commanded not to marry a Canaanite, his servant was sent out to find a suitable bride. Rebekah, according to the Joseph Smith Translation of Genesis 24:16, was described as being unlike any other: "And the damsel was very fair to look upon, a virgin, neither had any man known the like unto her." The servant was greatly impressed and brought her back to Isaac, who was also very pleased, "and he loved her" (Genesis 24:67). Rebekah proved to be a worthy companion, comforting Isaac after his mother's death, bearing the twins Jacob and Esau, and providing wisdom and counsel to her husband (see Genesis 24, 25).

**5. EVE**—The first of all women, the Mother of All Living. Clearly, she brightened Adam's world, and he seemed utterly delighted when she appeared on the scene (see Moses 3:23–24). Of course, Eve being the only woman on earth didn't give Adam much of a basis of comparison, and despite future fathers' advice to not marry the first girl you date, Adam had no choice. But Eve seemed to be a great catch. She wanted greater wisdom, sought to be modest once she realized she was naked, and proved to be handy with sewing fig leaves. Adam was so fond of her that he ate the fruit and knowingly risked being tossed out of the Garden of Eden because he wanted to continue to be with her. Also, once they were in the real world, Eve showed that she wasn't afraid to work: "And Eve, also, his wife, did labor with him" (Moses 5:1). A great catch indeed!

**4. RUTH**—This woman had both beauty and character. Her attractiveness is evident in the attention she received from Boaz. *Wow, who is this gleaning in my fields?* he must have thought. Boaz not only insisted that Ruth continue in his fields but then also offered her water, invited her to join him for a hot lunch date, and had his men purposely leave some of the good harvest for her. Ultimately, Boaz married Ruth and declared of her, "All the city of my people doth know that thou art a virtuous woman" (Ruth 3:11). Her character shone through in how well she treated her widowed mother-in-law, Naomi. As the Bible Dictionary puts it, "The story of Ruth beautifully illustrates the conversion of a non-Israelite into the fold of Israel, giving up her former god and former life to unite with the household of faith in the service of the God of Israel."

**3. SARAH**—Sarah, the wife of Abraham, whose name means "princess," was so attractive that Abraham asked her to pretend to be his sister when they went to Egypt so he wouldn't be killed for having such a desirable wife! "I know that thou art a fair woman to look upon," Abraham said to her before revealing his plan. Sure enough, they went into Egypt, and "the Egyptians beheld the woman that she was very fair." So they took her to Pharaoh's house, and her "brother" was given gifts of sheep, oxen,

donkeys, men and women servants, and camels in the hope that he would give Sarah's hand to Pharaoh. But "the Lord plagued Pharaoh and his house with great plagues" for trying to woo Sarah until the Egyptian ruler finally learned that Sarah was actually Abraham's wife. Then the Pharaoh sent them away unharmed and with many gifts and wealth. That's how impressed a pharaoh of Egypt was with the stunning beauty of Sarah. (See Genesis 12)

**2. RACHEL**—The runner-up in our rankings, Rachel had a biblical name that meant "ewe," and boy was this little lamb in hot demand in her suitor Jacob's eyes. She was described in Genesis as "beautiful and well favored" (29:17), and Jacob was so smitten that he kissed her on their first date at

the well. Who cared that they were cousins? Jacob was so thrilled to have found Rachel (and she was apparently such a remarkable kisser) that immediately after the embrace, he "lifted up his voice, and wept" (v. 11). Wow. When Rachel's father, Laban, hired Jacob and asked him what his wages should be, Jacob promptly replied, "I will serve thee seven years for Rachel thy younger daughter" (v. 18). Laban agreed. "And Jacob served seven years for Rachel; and they seemed unto him but a few days, for the love he had for her" (v. 20). Aww. Isn't that sweet?

But not wanting the younger sister married off before the older one, Laban gave Jacob the hand of Rachel's older sister, Leah, at the end of Jacob's seven years of labor. Laban then insisted that Jacob work seven *more* years for Rachel, which he did. Jacob was clearly devoted to the stunning beauty

**VALUE THE VIRTUOUS WOMAN!** "WHO CAN FIND A VIRTUOUS WOMAN? FOR HER PRICE IS FAR ABOVE RUBIES."
PROVERB 31:10

Rachel: "And Jacob said unto Laban, Give me my wife, for my days are fulfilled, that I may go in unto her" (v. 21).

Rachel eventually bore Jacob two precious sons, Joseph and Benjamin, though the difficult labor with Benjamin caused Rachel to die in childbirth. No wonder Jacob was so protective and favoring of Joseph and Benjamin for the rest of his life. They were living reminders of his dear, sweet Rachel.

**1. ESTHER**—Esther's Hebrew name was Hadassah, meaning "myrtle," but in Persian, she was known as Esther. An orphan raised by her cousin Mordecai, "the maid was fair and beautiful." Among all the women of the Persian Empire in about 500 B.C., Esther became known as one of the loveliest. "And Esther obtained favour in the sight of all them that looked upon her" (Esther 2:15).

When the king of Persia, Ahasuerus (probably Xerxes I), called all the finest young women to the palace so he could find a new queen, Esther stood out to Hegai, the royal screener of all the pageant's contestants: "And the maiden pleased him, and she obtained kindness of him . . . and he preferred her" and gave her "the best place of the house of women" (Esther 2:9). After she spent a year of purification and preparation among the other young women, it was time for Esther to be presented to the king. The chamberlains and maidservants who had been working with her were thrilled with their work and felt that with the beautiful Esther, the odds were ever in their favor. But would she be named Miss Persia? Would the king find her to be the fairest of them all?

**YOU'RE BOTH IN THIS TOGETHER, REMEMBER!** "NEVERTHELESS, NEITHER IS THE MAN WITHOUT THE WOMAN, NEITHER THE WOMAN WITHOUT THE MAN, IN THE LORD." 1 CORINTHIANS 11:11

Of course he did! "And the king loved Esther above all the women, and she obtained grace and favour in his sight more than all the virgins; so that he set the royal crown upon her head, and made her queen instead of Vashti" (Esther 2:17). Not only did this gal have the looks, but she had the pluck and bravery to later save the Jews from the evil Haman. In the words of the Bible Dictionary, Esther's heroism exhibits "a very high type of courage, loyalty, and patriotism." Esther had the complete package: incredibly good looks, backbone and soul, and spirituality and loyalty. This queen is the ultimate beauty of the Bible!

# *Three*
# BIG
# BOATS

Guys love their boats. Maybe it's the memories of fishing with Grandpa in a boat on a calm mountain lake or waterskiing in a reservoir with friends. Or maybe it is that we have visions of how cool we would be captaining a big ship (like Russell Crowe in *Master and Commander*) or feeling the luxury and power that navigating a yacht on the open sea would surely bring.

The scriptures are filled with boats of all sizes as well as an ocean of maritime references. Let's explore a few!

## NOAH'S ARK

When the Lord commanded Noah to build an ark, He instructed him to build a ship larger than any known boat in his era, anywhere in the world. In fact, no ships of this size were seen again for thousands of years. "And this is the fashion which thou shalt make it of: The length

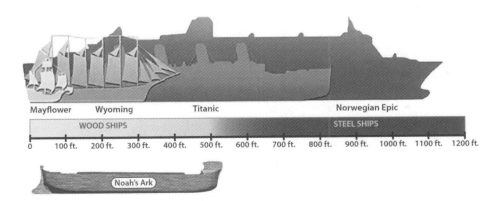

of the ark shall be three hundred cubits [450 feet], the breadth of it fifty cubits [75 feet], and the height of it thirty cubits [45 feet]" (Genesis 6:15).

This easily puts Noah's ark in the megayacht class. Such dimensions would allow for tremendous cargo, the equivalent of 522 boxcars. In raw dimensions, Noah's ark totals 129,000 cubic feet, and even factoring a hull wall and deck timbers of 1 foot thick, that leaves an interior space of 114,000 cubic feet.

In Genesis 6:14, we find additional details about this mammoth craft. The Lord said, "Make thee an ark of gopher wood." The Bible Dictionary describes gopher wood (coming from the Hebrew word *gophar* and completely unrelated to the small American mammal) as "the wood of a resin-yielding conifer, probably the cypress." The wood of a cypress tree is very durable and pleasantly scented. The doors of St. Peter's Basilica in Vatican City were made of cypress wood because of its protection and strength.

Noah was instructed further: "Rooms shalt thou make in the ark" (Genesis 6:14), which the footnotes tell us are actually "nests" or "compartments." This is logical, considering the varied cargo the ark held.

"And shalt pitch it within and without with pitch" (v. 14), the Lord directed. Pitch had long been used to caulk the seams of wooden sailing vessels, and considering the amount of water headed Noah's way, it seemed prudent to seal up the ark both "within and without." "A window shalt thou make to the ark, and in a cubit shalt thou finish it above," the Lord said (v. 14). If we think of this as a traditional window, this verse doesn't make much sense. Why would the Lord want just one window on a 450-foot-long ship? How could one window provide light and ventilation for the entire ship? In the footnotes of that verse, we read that *window* was translated from the Hebrew word *tsohar*, which means "light." The footnote adds, "Some rabbis believed it was a precious stone that shone in the ark." Indeed, some Jewish traditions describe the *tsohar* as a glowing jewel emanating God's light.[16] Perhaps

---

16 See Amy Eilberg, "Finding Light in Shadow of Darkness," J.weekly.com, Oct. 18,

this shining stone that lit the ark was what inspired the brother of Jared a mere 100 years or so after the flood to use stones to light his own ship. Another interpretation is that since *tsohar* means "light," the verse could simply be translated as, "Thou shalt make light for the ark," with the window sizes being dictated as a square cubit.[17]

Then the Lord prescribed, "And the door of the ark shalt thou set in the side thereof" (Genesis 6:14), and the ark should have "lower, second, and third stories" (v. 16). The idea of multiple floors on a ship—unheard of in Bronze Age vessels—was divinely inspired, as Noah would need room for his tremendous cargo.

Regarding passengers, the Lord directed, "Into the ark, thou, and thy sons [Shem, Ham, and Japheth], and thy wife, and thy sons' wives with thee" (v. 18). The first chapter in the book of Abraham tells us Ham's wife's name was Egyptus, but we don't know the names of the other women on board. However, 12 percent of Americans in a recent survey believe that Joan of Arc was Noah's wife's name![18]

Regarding animals, Noah was told, "Of every clean beast thou shalt take to thee by sevens, the male and his female: and of beasts that are not clean by two, the male and the female" (Genesis 7:2). So who were these animals Noah took on this massive ship?

Quite simply, the clean beasts described in the Old Testament and taken aboard the ark in sevens were those fit for sacrifices (cattle, oxen,

1996, http://www.jweekly.com/article/full/4275/noah-finding-light-in-shadow-of-darkness/.

17 Eric Lyons, "The 'Window' of the Ark," *Apologetic Press*, accessed January 27, 2014, https://www.apologeticspress.org/apcontent.aspx?category=6&article=1466.

18 Stephen Prothero, "A Nation of Faith and Religious Illiterates," *Los Angeles Times*, Jan. 12, 2005, http://articles.latimes.com/2005/jan/12/opinion/oe-prothero12.

goat, gazelle, antelope, sheep, etc.). The unclean beasts included those not fit for sacrifices (swine, camels, rabbits, rock badgers, mice, bats, chameleons, etc.). Biblical scholars such as Robert Best point out that this could mean there were fewer than 280 animals on the ark.

> How many kinds of clean animals were there? We don't have to guess. Deuteronomy 14:4–5 lists 10 species of clean animals, which implies 140 clean animals in Noah's barge. Assuming a minimum average of 12 square feet per animal (cramped but adequate), 1,680 square feet of deck area would be needed.

> How much deck area was needed for the unclean animals and birds? Leviticus 11:4–19 and Deuteronomy 14:7–18 list about 30 species of unclean animals and birds. Thirty pairs would be 60 animals. These small animals would fit in 2-feet by 2-feet cages. In addition, seven pairs of each of the five species of clean birds is a total of 70 clean birds. Assuming 4 square feet for each caged small animal and bird, only 520 square feet were needed. Thus the total deck area required for the estimated 270 animals was only 2,200 square feet, leaving plenty of deck area for walkways and baskets of grain piled several deep.

> Would it be practical for Noah, his wife, and his sons and their wives to feed and water 270 animals and haul out manure each day? Best points out that the logistics of tending to such a herd were also realistic: "Assuming 10 hour work days (not including rest and dinner breaks) each person would have 20 minutes per animal each day. Entirely practical.[19]

The Bible says nothing about polar bears, penguins, giraffes, kangaroos, orangutans, or pandas. It is perhaps, then, more logical to read the line "of every living thing of all flesh" as the biblically specified animals and not as all 8.7 million species on the planet. Brigham Young University zoologists Clayton M. White and Mark D. Thomas agree and point out, "The ark contained insufficient space to house every bird species,

19 Robert M. Best, *Noah's Ark* (Fort Meyers, Florida: Enlil Press, 1999), excerpted here: "Noah's Ark Had Less Than 280 Animals," http://www.noahs-ark-flood.com/animals.htm.

let alone mammals, reptiles, insects, plants, and other life forms."[20] Surely the menagerie on Noah's ark included goats, sheep, and chickens and not the anaconda, koalas, and freshwater river dolphins.

"It is doubtful whether the water in the sky and all the oceans would suffice to cover the earth so completely," Apostle (and chemist) John A. Widtsoe said of the literalist view of Noah's ark having specimens of every creature in the entire world, because the entire globe was to be submerged. "In fact, the details of the flood are not known to us," he continued, reminding us that "the scriptures must be read intelligently."[21] It is also important to remember that the word for *earth* in the Flood account in Genesis 7 is translated from the Hebrew word *eretz*. Most scholars agree that *eretz* is more accurately translated as "land," as in the "land of Israel," and *not* "earth," as in the whole planet, which modern readers might infer.[22]

When it says it rained for "forty days and forty nights" (Genesis 10:10) "and the flood was forty days upon the earth" (Genesis 7:17), it should be noted that "forty days and forty nights" is an idiom in Hebrew meaning "an indeterminably long time."[23] Moses may have fasted for fewer than 40 actual days, for example, and the great Flood may have lasted longer. At any rate, Noah and his family and the animals were aboard this big boat for a long, historic voyage.

**SAILORS SHOULD SING PRAISES TO GOD**
"SING UNTO THE LORD A NEW SONG, AND HIS PRAISE FROM THE END OF THE EARTH, YE THAT GO DOWN TO THE SEA, AND ALL THAT IS THEREIN; THE ISLES, AND THE INHABITANTS THEREOF."
ISAIAH 42:10

Regardless of the details of the Flood and the ark—and there are plenty of varying views by LDS

---

20 Clayton M. White and Mark D. Thomas, "On Balancing Faith in Mormonism with Traditional Biblical Stories: The Noachian Flood Story," *Dialogue: A Journal of Mormon Thought*, vol. 40, no. 3, 91.

21 John A. Widtsoe, *Evidences and Reconciliation: Aids to Faith in a Modern Day*, vol. 1 (Salt Lake City: Bookcraft, 1943), 109–110, 112.

22 Brian Bull and Fritz Guy, "The Genesis Account: Six Words Make All the Difference," *Spectrum*, Nov. 11, 2012, http://spectrummagazine.org/node/4870.

23 In Justin Deering, *The End-of-the-World" Delusion: How Doomsdayers Endanger Society* (Bloomington, IN: iUniverse), 8.

scholars and leaders through the years—the important thing is that prophet-sailor Noah and his righteous, obedient family were blessed for following the commandments of God: "And thus Noah found grace in the eyes of the Lord; for Noah was a just man, and perfect in his generation; and he walked with God, as did also his three sons, Shem, Ham, and Japheth" (Moses 8:27).

**WERE THE JAREDITES BLACK?** IT IS IMPORTANT TO NOTE THAT THE PEOPLE OF BABEL AND THE PLAINS OF SHINAR WERE NOT THE LIGHTER-SKINNED SEMITIC RACE (SHEMITIC, OR DESCENDANTS OF NOAH'S SON SHEM). RATHER, THEY WERE THE DARK-SKINNED HAMITIC PEOPLES, DESCENDANTS OF EGYPTUS, CUSH, AND NIMROD. IT DOESN'T MATTER THAT THE ARNOLD FRIBERG PAINTING SHOWS THE BROTHER OF JARED WITH WHITE SKIN; THE GENEALOGY OF THE BIBLE, THE HAMITIC NAMES OF THE JAREDITES, AND THE NEGROID FEATURES ON THE OLMEC HEADS OF JAREDITE-ERA MESOAMERICA SUGGEST THAT THE JAREDITES WERE BLACK.‡ THIS LIKELIHOOD PROVIDES FURTHER DEPTH AND MEANING TO THE STATEMENT IN THE TITLE PAGE OF THE BOOK OF MORMON THAT THE BOOK DEMONSTRATES THAT "JESUS IS THE CHRIST, THE ETERNAL GOD, MANIFESTING HIMSELF UNTO *ALL* NATIONS" (EMPHASIS ADDED).

## JAREDITE BARGES

Among the children of Noah's middle son, Ham, and his wife, Egyptus, was Cush, who is described in the Bible Dictionary as father of "the dark-skinned race." The tenth chapter of Genesis says, "And Cush begat Nimrod: he began to be a mighty one in the earth" (v. 8). Nimrod "was a mighty hunter before the Lord: wherefore it is said, Even as Nimrod the mighty hunter before the Lord" (v. 9). This great hunter and

‡ See "Were the Jaredites Black?" The Black Mormon Homepage accessed January 23, 2014, http://www.angelfire.com/mo2/blackmormon/JAREDITES.html.

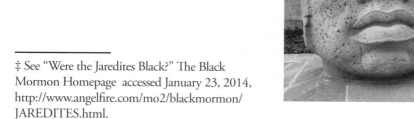

great-grandson of Noah became the founder of Babel and other cities on the plains of Shinar.

Some of Nimrod's posterity in Babel were wicked and began to build a tower to get to heaven—presumably an easier method than repentance and obedience. But others in Babel, such as Jared and his brother Mahonri Moriancumer, were righteous and successfully obtained from the Lord the blessings of not having their language confounded and being led to a promised land.

Noah's ark may be known for its size and colorful cargo, but the Jaredite barges stand out for their agility. The barges were built "according to the instructions of the Lord" and "after the manner of barges which ye have hitherto built" (Ether 2:16). We learn here that the Jaredites gained some experience building barges after they first left Babel and as they crossed many waters while they traveled in the wilderness (see Ether 2:6).

Noah used pitch to seal the timbers of the ark, and the Jaredite barges may have been similarly sealed, for "they were exceedingly tight, even that they would hold water like unto a dish; and the bottom thereof was tight like unto a dish; and the sides thereof were tight like unto a dish . . . and the door thereof, when it was shut, was tight like unto a dish" (Ether 2:17).

Like Noah, they also had animals aboard: "Their flocks and herds, and whatsoever beast or animal or fowl that they should carry with them . . . got aboard of their vessels or barges" (Ether 6:4).

The barges were practically required to be ancient submarines at times. "Ye shall be as a whale in the midst of the sea; for the mountain waves shall dash upon you" (Ether 2:24). "They were many times buried in the depths of the sea" (Ether 6:6). "When they were buried in the deep there was no water that could hurt them, their vessels being tight like unto a dish, and also they were tight like unto the ark of Noah" (Ether 6:7). "And no monster of the sea could break them, neither whale that could mar them" (Ether 6:10).

Without oars or sails, the Jaredite barges were powered by the winds and currents of the sea. The scriptures state, "The Lord God caused that there should be a furious wind . . . and thus they were tossed upon the waves of the sea before the wind" (Ether 6:5). "The wind did never cease to blow . . . and thus they were driven . . . before the wind" (Ether 6:8). The Jaredites' remarkable trans-oceanic journey from Asia to the Americas took nearly a year—344 days. By comparison, with the added assistance of sail power, it took Columbus only 34 days to cross the Atlantic on his first voyage, and it took the crew of Ferdinand Magellan three years and one month to be the first to circumnavigate the globe, from 1519 to 1522.

President Spencer W. Kimball summarized the Jaredite epic in the book of Ether as follows:

> This unparalleled book should intrigue navigators: unprecedented land treks near-unbelievable in length, scope, and hazard are

chronicled and ocean crossings, and the circling of the world centuries before the Vikings—crossings fraught with all the dangers imaginable, including storms, hidden reefs, hurricanes, and even mutiny. This first recorded ocean crossing was about forty centuries ago, of seaworthy, ocean-going vessels without known sails, engines, oars, or rudders—eight barges like and near contemporary with Noah's ark, long as a tree, tight as a dish, peaked at the end like a gravy boat (see Ether 2:17), corked at top and bottom, illuminated by molten stones [see Ether 2:20; Ether 3:1ff.], perhaps with radium or some other substance not yet rediscovered by our scientists. Light and like a [fowl] upon the water, this fleet of barges was driven by winds and ocean currents, landing at a common point in North America probably on the west shores.[24]

## KING SOLOMON'S NAVY

Let's fast forward to more than 1,000 years after the Flood and the Tower of Babel and stop at 1015 B.C. King David died that year in Jerusalem, and his son Solomon was crowned king of Israel. Until Solomon's death forty years later in 975 B.C., Israel enjoyed a Golden Age that saw the biblical kingdom reach its zenith. Solomon ruled in wisdom, built a temple, and the boundaries of the realm stretched from the coasts of the Mediterranean east

to Salecah in the Syrian desert and from Kadesh north of Lebanon south to the port of Ezion-geber on the Red Sea's Gulf of Aqaba. With a kingdom touching the shores of both the Mediterranean and the Red Sea, King Solomon wisely organized a navy. This was less of a fighting navy, as we may think of when we hear the word, and more of a fleet of dominating trade ships.

We read in 1 Kings 9:26: "And king Solomon made a navy of ships in Ezion-geber, which is beside Eloth, on the shore of the Red sea,

---

24 *Conference Report*, April 1963, 63–64.

THE KINGDOM OF
DAVID AND SOLOMON

— Greatest extent of the empire

Territory conquered by David

- - - Territory under economic influence of Solomon

in the land of Edom," and in 1 Kings 9:27: "And Hiram sent in the navy his servants, shipmen that had knowledge of the sea, with the servants of Solomon." This Hiram, of course, was King Hiram I of Tyre, which he had developed into the most important Phoenician city. Hiram had forged a mutually beneficial relationship with King David and continued the association with Solomon. By the time Solomon began to reign, the Phoenicians had become some of the finest sailors and explorers in the ancient world, and Hiram's shipmen most likely had great knowledge to impart to the Israelite navy.

Solomon and Hiram worked together to build trade routes throughout the Red Sea and beyond into the Arabian Sea: "And they came to Ophir, and fetched from thence gold, four hundred and twenty talents, and brought it to king Solomon" (1 Kings 9:28; see also 2 Chronicles 8:17–18). The trade with Ophir was a key source of Solomon's enormous wealth, and many scholars identify the ancient port of Sopara near modern-day Mumbai, India, as Ophir.[25] Tradesmen brought gold, silver, ivory, exotic apes, and beautiful peacocks to the court of King Solomon using the extensive trade networks, which ranged from the Indian subcontinent in the East to Tarshish (Tartessos) in southern Spain (see 2 Chronicles 9:21).

Solomon's ships would have used a sail and oars, like the Phoenician sailing galleys. With rows of oars, some ships had crews of more than

---

25 For example, see A. L. Bashman, *The Wonder That Was India* (London: Picador Press, 2005).

100. The vast, rounded hulls of the cargo ships helped maximize the treasure being brought back from long-distance voyages.

With such a fleet, the prophets could wax poetic about faraway lands. Isaiah said, "Surely the isles shall wait for me, and the ships of Tarshish first, to bring thy sons from far, their silver and their gold with them, unto the name of the Lord thy God, the Holy One of Israel, because he hath glorified thee" (Isaiah 60:9).

## JONAH'S SHIP

In the 700s B.C., about 300 years after the reign of Solomon and during the reign of King Jeroboam II, we find the prophet Jonah preaching. His story also involves a big boat.

The Lord said to Jonah, "Arise, go to Nineveh, that great city, and cry against it; for their wickedness is come up before me" (Jonah 1:2). Located on the banks of the Tigris River in what is now northern  Iraq, Nineveh was the capital of the Assyrian kingdom, the largest city in the world at the time,[26] and was so intimidating in size that it took three days just to walk through it.[27] It was proud, idolatrous, and ruthless in pursuing world domination. It was also outside the land of Israel, where Jonah and other prophets of his era were used to laboring.

"Nineveh?" Jonah must have balked. "Really?" Jonah wanted nothing of it. Rather than travel 500 miles east of his hometown of Gath-hepher, near

26 Mark T. Rosenburg, "Largest Cities through History," About.com Geography, accessed January 23, 2014, http://geography.about.com/library/weekly/aa011201a.htm.
27 See "Listen to the Prophets," *Ensign*, May 1978.

Nazareth, to get to Nineveh, Jonah headed west, in the opposite direction, to the coastal port of Joppa. "He found a ship going to Tarshish: so he paid the fare thereof, and went down into it, to go with them unto Tarshish from the presence of the Lord" (Jonah 1:3).

We can imagine Jonah at the seaport in Joppa, attempting to flee from the Lord. "What ship can take me farthest away from my doomed assignment to Nineveh?" he must have wondered. Boarding the ship to Tarshish was logical, as that destination, located on the Atlantic side of the Iberian Peninsula in modern Spain, was literally the end of the line for the ancient Israelite and Phoenician ships. It was, in the ancient Hebrews' view, the edge of the known world and a place modern scholars have said is the source of the legends of Atlantis. If you are fleeing from the God of Israel, sailing 2,500 miles across the entire Mediterranean Sea and through the Pillars of Hercules (as the ancients called the Strait of Gibraltar) would take you as far away as you could get. Or so Jonah thought.

The largest ships of that era were known as ships of Tarshish, even if they were going elsewhere. As the Bible Dictionary says, "The name came to be used to denote ships of the largest size, suitable for long voyages." Likewise, we use our largest airliners today for transoceanic flights. Jonah was aboard a larger ship of Tarshish because his destination was Tarshish itself. We know it was a larger vessel because while the men of the ship were praying to their various gods and casting overboard their excess wares to save the ship, "Jonah was gone down into the sides of the ship; and he lay, and was fast asleep" (Jonah 1:5). This implies that there were lower decks on the ship. Jonah's transport, in addition to sails, also had oars to help guide it like so many of the ancient ships: "Nevertheless the men rowed hard to bring it to the land; but they could not: for the sea wrought, and was tempestuous against them" (Jonah 1:13).

This must have been some storm to affect this enormous ship of Tarshish, the Boeing 747 jumbo jet of its day, to the point that "the ship was like to be broken" (Jonah 1:4).

President James E. Faust summarizes the rest of the story nicely:

> However, the Lord caused a mighty tempest to come upon the sea. The mariners were frightened, and in an effort to appease the Lord, they threw Jonah into the sea. A great fish swallowed Jonah, and he was in the belly of the fish for three days and three nights. Jonah prayed for forgiveness and deliverance, and the fish vomited him onto dry land. The second time the word of the Lord came to Jonah, he listened and went to call the people of Nineveh to repentance.[28]

## NEPHI'S SHIP

After Lehi's family reached the seashore, the Lord commanded Nephi, "Thou shalt construct a ship, after the manner which I shall show thee, that I may carry thy people across these waters" (1 Nephi 17:8). What kind of lumber was Nephi's ship made of? "Archaeologists estimate that four types of wood were being used in constructing vessels in this period of time and in this area," Professor Kelly DeVries of Loyola University Maryland says. "These were palm, teak, cedar, and mulberry. Palm and mulberry, and sometimes cedar, were grown in the region of southern Arabia." He points out that palm, while buoyant, would not have been sturdy enough for such a long voyage. Mulberry is the most likely candidate for Nephi's ship, with cedar and teak being other options.[29]

28 "Did You Get the Right Message?" *Ensign*, May 2004.
29 In "Journey of Faith: Ships," Maxwell Institute, accessed January 23, 2014, http://publications.maxwellinstitute.byu.edu/fullscreen/?pub=1142&index=7.

"And we did work timbers of curious workmanship," Nephi said. "And the Lord did show me from time to time after what manner I should work the timbers of the ship" (1 Nephi 18:1).

Nephi would have been somewhat familiar with ships, and since they reached the Gulf of Aqaba and then headed south, he would have seen Egyptian, Phoenician, and possibly Greek trading vessels come and go. But to cross a couple of oceans required more than the humble flat-bottomed trading ships of that ancient age. Nephi said, "Now I, Nephi, did not work the timbers after the manner which was learned by men, neither did I build the ship after the manner of men; but I did build it after the manner which the Lord had shown unto me; wherefore, it was not after the manner of men" (1 Nephi 18:2). Professor DeVries suggests that Nephi's ship was much like the transoceanic ships of Columbus's day, with a deep, tall hull that could withstand such a voyage and was therefore certainly not characteristic of the ships of Nephi's time, or of "the manner of men" in his day.

Nephi needed strong ropes and cords for such a ship and such a voyage. "There is a small dwarf palm that grows in the mountains of the Dhofar region of Oman that makes an excellent cordage," Brigham Young University Biology Professor Gary Baird points out. "One

## THE SAILOR'S PSALM

THEY THAT GO DOWN TO THE SEA IN SHIPS, THAT DO BUSINESS IN GREAT WATERS;

THESE SEE THE WORKS OF THE LORD, AND HIS WONDERS IN THE DEEP.

FOR HE COMMANDETH, AND RAISETH THE STORMY WIND, WHICH LIFTETH UP THE WAVES THEREOF.

THEY MOUNT UP TO THE HEAVEN, THEY GO DOWN AGAIN TO THE DEPTHS: THEIR SOUL IS MELTED BECAUSE OF TROUBLE.

THEY REEL TO AND FRO, AND STAGGER LIKE A DRUNKEN MAN, AND ARE AT THEIR WITS' END.

THEN THEY CRY UNTO THE LORD IN THEIR TROUBLE, AND HE BRINGETH THEM OUT OF THEIR DISTRESSES.

HE MAKETH THE STORM A CALM, SO THAT THE WAVES THEREOF ARE STILL.

THEN ARE THEY GLAD BECAUSE THEY BE QUIET; SO HE BRINGETH THEM UNTO THEIR DESIRED HAVEN.

OH THAT MEN WOULD PRAISE THE LORD FOR HIS GOODNESS, AND FOR HIS WONDERFUL WORKS TO THE CHILDREN OF MEN!

PSALMS 107:23–31

of the unique features of that particular type of rope is that unlike other ropes, which degrade when exposed to water, the dwarf palm rope actually strengthens and toughens when exposed to water."[30]

## PETER'S FISHING BOAT

Simon Peter and his family were fisherman, and their boat was the site of the miraculous catch of fish when they first met Jesus (see Luke 5:1–11). But what kind of boat was it? A typical Galilean fishing boat was found in 1986 near the shore of the Sea of Galilee, seemingly abandoned 2000 years ago after many decades of use. It is 27 feet long and 7.5 feet wide, has a keel, and is not simply flat bottomed. It fit a crew of 5 and up to 15 passengers. Because of its historic possibilities (or at least similarities to what Peter's actual boat must have been like), the vessel is affectionately known as the *Jesus Boat* and is proudly displayed in the Yigal Allon Museum in Israel today.[31]

---

30 In "Journey of Faith: Ships," Maxwell Institute, accessed January 23, 2014, http://publications.maxwellinstitute.byu.edu/fullscreen/?pub=1142&index=7.
31 This boat is the prized artifact at the Yigal Alon Center in Kibbutz Ginosar, Israel. See "The Galilee Boat," Israel: Come Find the Israel in You, accessed January 23, 2014, http://www.goisrael.com/Tourism_Eng/Tourist%20Information/Christian%20Themes/Details/Pages/The%20Galilee%20Boat.aspx.

## Four
# KILLER WEAPONS

Since the dark day when Cain slew Abel, the sons of Adam and the daughters of Eve have brandished weapons in order to fight and to defend themselves. Imagine if the most prominent weapons of the scriptures were gathered into one museum! The artifacts would be stunning, and the stories behind them legendary. Let's imagine what such an exhibit would include.

## SWORD OF LABAN

When Nephi came across passed-out-drunk Laban, the first thing Nephi noted was Laban's amazing sword: "And I drew it forth from the sheath thereof; and the hilt thereof was of pure gold, and the workmanship thereof was exceedingly fine, and I saw that the blade thereof was of the most precious steel" (1 Nephi 4:9).

But this is not just a pretty sword; this is a fighting sword. It became the blueprint for other Nephite swords (see 2 Nephi 5:14). It was also the sword the early Nephite kings personally used in battle against the Lamanites; these kings included Nephi himself (see Jacob 1:10) and King Benjamin (see Words of Mormon 1:13). This kingly heirloom was passed down through generations and was clearly an important royal Nephite relic (see Mosiah 1:16).

The Three Witnesses to the gold plates were promised in June 1829 that they would get to see this famous sword (see D&C 17:1), and David Whitmer reported that this happened "in the latter part of the month."[32]

---

32 Andrew Jenson, *Historical Record*, vol. 6, nos. 3–5, May 1887, 208.

Two months before he died, Brigham Young revealed that Joseph Smith and Oliver Cowdery saw this Nephite national treasure on another occasion in a cave in the Hill Cumorah. The sword of Laban was unsheathed and lying on a table with these words written upon it: "This sword will never be sheathed again until the kingdoms of this world become the kingdom of our God and his Christ."[33]

## GOLIATH'S SWORD & ARMOR

The largest artifacts in a hypothetical scriptural weapons museum would certainly be the weapons of the giant Goliath of Gath, whom David slew. Goliath was "six cubits and a span" tall (1 Samuel 17:4), translating to 9 feet 3 inches, or 2.82 meters tall.

"And he had an helmet of brass upon his head, and he was armed with a coat of mail; and the weight of the coat was five thousand shekels of brass [about 167 pounds]. And he had greaves of brass upon his legs [shin armor], and a target [*targum* or neck armor] of brass between his shoulders" (1 Samuel 17:5–6).

WAS THERE STEEL IN 600 B.C.? FROM THE EARLIEST CRITICS OF THE BOOK OF MORMON ON DOWN, NAYSAYERS HAVE ARGUED THAT "LABAN IS REPRESENTED AS KILLED BY ONE NEPHI, SOME SIX HUNDRED YEARS BEFORE CHRIST, WITH A SWORD 'OF THE MOST PRECIOUS STEEL,' HUNDREDS OF YEARS BEFORE STEEL WAS KNOWN TO MAN!"[‡] THE PROBLEM WITH SUCH CRITICISM IS THAT STEEL (AN ALLOY OF IRON WITH CARBON AND OTHER ELEMENTS) IS INCREASINGLY BEING DISCOVERED IN MODERN ARCHEOLOGICAL DIGS. NOT ONLY THROUGHOUT THE MEDITERRANEAN WORLD BUT EVEN IN PLACES CLOSE TO JERUSALEM, LIKE GALILEE AND JERICHO, ANCIENT STEEL WEAPONS ARE BEING FOUND. LABAN'S AMAZING STEEL SWORD IS NOT SO FARFETCHED AFTER ALL![‡‡]

[33] *Journal of Discourses*, 19:38.

[‡] Daniel Bartlett, *The Mormons or, Latter-day Saints: Whence Came They?* (Cambridge, MA: Queen's College, 1911), 15. See other criticisms and defenses about steel in the Book of Mormon online at Fair Mormon Blog, http://blog.fairmormon.org/2013/06/17/labans-sword-of-most-precious-steel-howlers-5-2/.

[‡‡] Robert Maddin, James D. Muhly, and Tamara S. Wheeler, "How the Iron Age Began," *Scientific American* 237/4 [October 1977]:127; see also Amihai Mazar, *Archaeology of the Land of the Bible 10,000–586 B.C.E.* (New York: Doubleday, 1990), 361; see also Hershall Shanks, "Antiquities Director Confronts Problems and Controversies," *Biblical Archaeology Review* 12/4 [July–August 1986]: 33, 35.

**GOLIATH'S SWORD IN IRELAND?**
SOME LEGENDS TELL OF THE TRIBE OF DAN ULTIMATELY IMMIGRATING TO IRELAND AS THE PROMINENT BUT MYSTERIOUS TUATHA DE DANANN OF IRISH HISTORY. SOME BELIEVE THE TRIBE OF DAN BROUGHT THE SWORD OF GOLIATH WITH THEM TO THE EMERALD ISLE.‡‡‡

Goliath also had a giant spear: "And the staff of his spear was like a weaver's beam; and his spear's head weighed six hundred shekels of iron [about 20 pounds]: and one bearing a shield went before him" (1 Samuel 17:7). Some biblical scholars conclude that Goliath's spear was 26 feet long.[34] These were huge weapons and were clearly intimidating to the Israelites.

David's first encounter with Goliath's sword was after the smooth stone from his sling knocked out the boasting Philistine: "Therefore David ran, and stood upon the Philistine, and took his sword, and drew it out of the sheath thereof, and slew him, and cut off his head therewith. And when the Philistines saw their champion was dead, they fled" (1 Samuel 17:51).

Goliath's giant sword was noteworthy for both its size and its outstanding crafts-manship, and David kept it for himself. He gave the head of Goliath to King Saul, "but he put his armor in his tent" (1 Samuel 17:54). The sword was treated as a kingly relic

---

34 See "The Sword and Spear of Goliath," Bible Study Site, biblestudy.org, accessed January 23, 2014, http://www.biblestudy.org/theplainertruth/what-happened-to-sword-and-spear-of-goliath.html.

‡‡‡ See "The *Mysterious Tribe of Dan," Hope of Israel Ministries,* accessed January 23, 2014, http://www.hope-of-israel.org/i000035a.htm.

and traveled about Israel behind the ephod, or ceremonial priestly robe, after that (see 1 Samuel 21:9).

## DAVID'S SLING

Related to Goliath's gear is the humble weapon that brought him down. David's sling was a common shepherd's weapon in the Near East and was popular in the Israelite militia. Made of leather or wool, the slings of David's day were about 3 feet long and had a simple pocket to hold a stone. In one smooth loop around the head, with an underhand release, the slinger could propel the projectile swiftly and accurately. Imagine a fast-pitch softball player—one swift wind-up is all that's needed.[35]

**HOW DEADLY IS A SLING? A SIMPLE SLING CAN THROW A SMOOTH ROCK OVER 400 METERS AND EXCEED 60 MILES PER HOUR! THE DEADLY ACCURACY OF THIS WEAPON INSPIRED THE ISRAEL DEFENSE FORCES TO NAME THEIR NEW MISSILE DEFENSE SYSTEM DAVID'S SLING, IN ITS HONOR. THE SYSTEM IS SCHEDULED TO BE OPERATIONAL BY 2015.**

---

35 For more information see Chris Harrison, "The Sling in Medieval Europe," *The Bulletin of Primitive Technology* 31 (Spring 2006); see also Yigael Yadin, *The Art of Warfare in Biblical Lands* (Jerusalem: International Publishing Company, 1963), 34–35; see also "David's Sling and Stone: Were They Toys or Weapons," Christiananswers.net, accessed January 23, 2014, http://www.christiananswers.net/q-abr/abr-slingsforkids.html.

Smooth, round stones went the farthest, so it was not uncommon for men to gather smooth stones from a riverbed and place them in their bags for later. "And David put his hand in his bag, and took thence a stone, and slang it, and smote the Philistine in his forehead, that the stone sunk into his forehead; and he fell upon his face to the earth. So David prevailed over the Philistine with a sling and with a stone, and smote the Philistine and slew him" (1 Samuel 17:49–50).

## FLOATING AX

The ax is seen as a weapon more in the Book of Mormon than in the Bible. The Lamanites were skilled in the ax for warfare, and from Enos to Mormon, writers pointed out its use (see Enos 1:20; Mormon 6:9). But perhaps the most curious ax in the scriptures is the floating ax associated with the prophet Elisha: "But as one was felling a beam, the axe head fell into the water: and he cried, and said, Alas, master! for it was borrowed. And the man of God said, Where fell it? And he shewed him the place. And he cut down a stick, and cast it in thither; and the iron did swim. Therefore said he, Take it up to thee. And he put out his hand, and took it" (2 Kings 6:5–7).

Elisha was using the sacred River Jordan to once again demonstrate to the people that he was a prophet. He had already split the waters of the river with Elijah's coat and walked through on dry land, and he had already instructed Naaman, the Syrian captain, to wash away his leprosy in the Jordan River. But a floating ax head? Now that is cool.

**BATTLE AX OR SWORD?** THE BATTLE AX IS MORE EFFECTIVE AGAINST ARMOR THAN THE SWORD BECAUSE THE WEIGHT OF THE AX HEAD IS CONCENTRATED INTO A SMALLER TARGET AREA, RESULTING IN MORE CLEAVING POWER THAN A SWORD AND CAUSING MORE DAMAGE TO THE ARMED ENEMY. AXES WERE CONSIDERABLY MORE COMMON IN THE ANCIENT WORLD THAN SWORDS AND DOUBLED AS TOOLS AND WEAPONS.

Iron was a rare commodity in ancient Israel, so having it float back up to the man who borrowed it saved him from a steep debt he would have owed had he lost it for good.

## CIMETERS

Enos talked about the Lamanite skill with the cimeter (see Enos 1:20), and it appears that this weapon was originally Lamanitish in origin. But by Zeniff's time, his Nephite group was so desperate for defense against the Lamanites that they adopted the cimeter and anything else they could think of: "And it came to pass that I did arm them with bows, and with arrows, with swords, and with cimeters, and with clubs, and with slings, and with all manner of weapons which we could invent, and I and my people did go forth against the Lamanites to battle" (Mosiah 9:16).

After that point, the cimeter appeared as a useful weapon for both Nephites and Lamanites throughout the many subsequent battles in the Book of Mormon and was usually mentioned alongside swords as a tool for slicing and hacking: "And the work of death commenced on both sides, but it was more dreadful on the part of the Lamanites, for their nakedness was exposed to the heavy blows of the Nephites with their swords and their cimeters, which brought death at almost every stroke" (Alma 43:37).

Yikes! Not mentioned in other lists of weapons

The Sword of Goliath

Sword of Laban

Roman Gladius

Aztec Macuahuitl

Mayan Macuahuitl

in battles after the coming of Christ, perhaps the cimeter fell out of use, but it appeared to be brutally effective while they had it.

*Cimeter* is an old spelling of *scimitar*, which today is identified largely as a sword that is sharp on one side only and is usually curved. Some Brigham Young University scholars conclude that "the Book of Mormon cimeter should probably be identified with a curved, axlike weapon held by many of the figures in the Temple of the Warriors at Chichen Itza. It appears to be a curved piece of wood in the end of which was inserted obsidian or flint blades."[36]

Is PETER'S SWORD IN POLAND? THE POZNAŇ ARCHDIOCESAN MUSEUM IN POLAND HAS A WIDE-TIPPED, MACHETE-LIKE SWORD 27.6 INCHES LONG AND MADE FROM A SINGLE PIECE OF IRON. THEY CLAIM IT IS THE SWORD PETER USED TO DEFEND THE LORD. THE RELIC ARRIVED AS A GIFT IN 968 FROM POPE JOHN XIII TO BISHOP JORDAN, FIRST BISHOP OF POLAND. RESEARCH COMPLETED IN 2005 BY SCIENTISTS AT THE POLISH ARMY MUSEUM IN WARSAW SHOWS THAT THE SWORD COULD BE FROM THE EASTERN ROMAN EMPIRE ABOUT 2,000 YEARS AGO, THOUGH IT IS IMPOSSIBLE TO AUTHENTICATE IF IT WAS ACTUALLY PETER'S.[‡]

## PETER'S SWORD

Remember the days when the senior member of the Twelve used to carry around a sword? Peter did. In fact, he used his sword to cut off the right ear of Malchus, the servant of the Jewish high priest Caiaphas, who was part of the mob coming to arrest the Savior in Gethsemane: "And Jesus answered and said, Suffer ye thus far. And he touched his ear, and healed him" (Luke 22:50). It was not uncommon for men in that era to carry around a sword, dagger, or Roman gladius.

---

36 William J. Hamblin and A. Brent Merrill, "Warfare in the Book of Mormon: Notes on the Cimeter (Scimitar) in the Book of Mormon," Maxwell Institute, accessed January 23, 2014, http://publications.maxwellinstitute.byu.edu/fullscreen/?pub=1108&index=17.

‡Tajemnice Ostrowa Tumskiego. Kraków: Zysk i S-ka, June 19, 2006, http://poznan.naszemiasto.pl/artykul/185833,janasowi-dziekujemy,id,t.html.

# CORIANTUMR'S SWORD

Beheading someone with a sword is not an easy task. It would need to be a clean, two-handed blow with a very sharp sword, preferably between the cricoid and thyroid cartilages in the neck, avoiding the bones of the vertebrae as much as possible. This is why the French resorted to a guillotine in their revolution. But we do have a few instances of decapitation in the scriptures, and Goliath's and Laban's swords weren't the only ones used to behead somebody. In the final, exhausting battle between Coriantumr and Shiz, the two surviving Jaredite leaders, Coriantumr leaned on his sword to rest and then "smote off the head of Shiz" (Ether 15:30).

Now, Shiz's decapitated body did an interesting thing: "And it came to pass that after he had smitten off the head of Shiz, that Shiz raised up on his hands and fell; and after that he had struggled for breath, he died" (Ether 15:31).

## METHUSELAH'S "WONDERFUL SWORD"

THE ANCIENT PATRIARCH METHUSELAH IS KNOWN IN JEWISH TRADITION FOR HAVING A "WONDERFUL SWORD" THAT HE USED TO SLAY EVIL DEMONS. THE MIRACULOUS SWORD OF METHUSELAH WAS SUPPOSEDLY PASSED DOWN TO ABRAHAM, ISAAC, AND JACOB AND WAS DESCRIBED AS BEING "MORE PRECIOUS THAN MONEY."‡

The common phrase "running around like a chicken with your head cut off" comes to mind. The reality is that poultry often will keep running around after their head is cut off, as the adrenaline and blood keep pumping for a time and the muscle memory reacts. The same results occur with rats and other mammals. One Dutch rat study showed the rats' bodies moving about 4 seconds after decapitation, and other studies have shown small mammals moving up to 29 seconds after losing their heads.[37] Additionally, during the French Revolution, bodies would notably twitch after the guillotine removed their head, so Shiz's brainless reaction is realistic after all. The exposed trachea gasping for breath in the midst of a headless neck would be a gruesome sight though.

---

37 See Josh Clark, "Do You Really Stay Conscious after Being Decapitated?" howstuffworks.com, accessed January 23, 2014, http://science.howstuffworks.com/science-vs-myth/extrasensory-perceptions/lucid-decapitation3.htm.

## AMMON'S SWORD

So you think you have the right to bear arms? Ammon may disagree with you. A leader in ancient American disarmament, he had the strength and skill to defend King Lamoni's flock in a memorable way: "But behold, every man that lifted his club to smite Ammon, he smote off their arms with his sword; for he did withstand their blows by smiting their arms with the edge of his sword, insomuch that they began to be astonished, and began to flee before him; yea and they were not few in number; and he caused them to flee by the strength of his arm" (Alma 17:37).

Chopping off enemies' arms was not uncommon in ancient America. "Cutting off an enemy's arm in battle not only rendered him utterly helpless but also netted the victor a grisly trophy to carry from the scene of battle that would validate his prowess in hand-to-hand combat," researcher Bruce H. Yerman noted. "Documents from Mexico and Guatemala reveal such a pre-Columbian custom."[38]

Ammon didn't just amputate an arm or two, which would have been impressive in itself, but he took off a whole bunch of them: "He smote off as many of their arms as were lifted against him, and they were not a few" (Alma 17:38). King Lamoni was so stunned at the feat that he thought Ammon was a god. To cut off that many arms required Ammon to have great strength and skill, divine guidance, and one amazing sword.

---

38 Bruce H. Yerman, "Ammon and the Mesoamerican Custom of Smiting off Arms," *Journal of Book of Mormon Studies*: vol. 8, no. 1 (Provo, Utah: Maxwell Institute, 1999): 46.

‡ Louis Ginzberg, *The Legends of the Jews*, 7 vols. (Philadelphia: The Jewish Publication Society of America, 1913—25), 1:141, 1:321, 5:165.

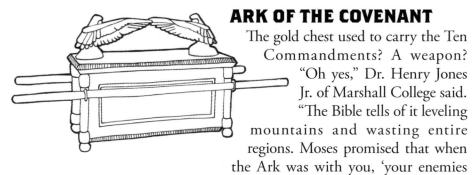

## ARK OF THE COVENANT

The gold chest used to carry the Ten Commandments? A weapon? "Oh yes," Dr. Henry Jones Jr. of Marshall College said. "The Bible tells of it leveling mountains and wasting entire regions. Moses promised that when the Ark was with you, 'your enemies will be scattered and your foes fell before you.'" Dr. Jones continued. "An army which carries the Ark before it is invincible."[39]

Indeed, in some respects, the ark of the covenant was the most powerful weapon in the scriptures. The Israelites used it in a number of battles. They conquered the city of Jericho after they carried the ark around the city seven times. Then the "people shouted with a great shout," and the walls came tumbling down (Joshua 6:20). They also carried the ark into battle successfully against the Ammonites (see 2 Samuel 11).

**WHERE SHOULD RAIDERS OF THE LOST ARK LOOK TODAY?** THE ETHIOPIAN ORTHODOX CHURCH CLAIMS TO HAVE THE ARK OF THE COVENANT HIDDEN AND UNDER GUARD IN THE CHURCH OF OUR LADY MARY OF ZION IN AKSUM, ETHIOPIA.[‡] THE LEMBA PEOPLE OF SOUTH AFRICA AND ZIMBABWE CLAIM THAT THEIR ANCESTORS CARRIED THE ARK FARTHER SOUTH AND BURIED IT IN A CAVE IN THE DUMGHE MOUNTAINS.[‡‡] SOME RESEARCHERS SPECULATE THAT THE KNIGHTS TEMPLAR IN THE MIDDLE AGES BROUGHT THE ARK TO WARWICKSHIRE, ENGLAND, TO CHARTRES CATHEDRAL IN FRANCE, OR TO THE SOUTHERN FRENCH VILLAGE OF RENNES-LE-CHÂTEAU,[‡‡‡] AND THEN FREEMASONS BROUGHT IT TO THE UNITED STATES TO PROTECT IT DURING WORLD WAR I.

---

39 Lawrence Kasdan, *Raiders of the Lost Ark*, screenplay, Aug. 1979, http://www.dailyscript.com/scripts/RaidersoftheLostArk.pdf.

‡ See Paul Raffaele, "Keepers of the Lost Ark?" *Smithsonian Magazine*, Dec. 2007, http://www.smithsonianmag.com/people-places/keepers-of-the-lost-ark-179998820/.

‡‡ David Van Biema, "A Lead on the Ark of the Covenant," *Time Magazine*, Feb. 21, 2008, http://content.time.com/time/health/article/0,8599,1715337,00.html.

‡‡‡ Karen Ralls, *The Templars and The Grail: Knights of the Quest* (Wheaton, IL: Theosophical Publishing House, 2003), 99.

Once, the Philistines captured the ark for a season. King David built a special tent to protect it, and King Solomon kept it in the Holy of Holies in the temple at Jerusalem. But where did this sacred biblical weapon end up?

In the Apocrypha, it claims that all of the treasures of the king, including the "ark of God," were taken away into Babylon with the children of Israel (see 1 Esdras 1:54). Other apocryphal verses state that before the Babylonian captivity, the prophet Jeremiah hid the ark of the covenant in a cave in Mount Nebo, in today's country of Jordan (see 2 Maccabees 2:4–10). Either way, the ark of the covenant disappeared, and by New Testament times it was no longer on the scene.

# Five
# FAVORITE FUNNY VERSES

From teachers quorums to high priest groups, from seminary classes to the MTC, guys love sharing their favorite funny scriptures. Sometimes the verses are meant to have irony and humor, but often, it is all about taking the right verse and putting it in a different context. Here are a few to have some fun with next time you have to teach the deacons and want to liven things up.

Let's start with the Old Testament—a treasure trove of strange and humorous verses. Sports verses such as "In the big inning" and "Joseph served in Pharaoh's court" don't really exist, unfortunately, but enjoy what does:

### THE DAY FATHER ABRAHAM WAS REALLY UPSET!
Genesis 21:24—And Abraham said, I will swear.

### DID REBEKAH HAVE A SMOKING HABIT?
Genesis 24:64—And Rebekah lifted up her eyes, and when she saw Isaac, she lighted off the camel.

### BAD NEWS FOR GLINDA, ELPHABA, HERMIONE GRANGER, PROFESSOR MCGONAGALL, URSULA, ETC.
Exodus 22:18—Thou shalt not suffer a witch to live.

## AARON GIVES THE LAMEST EXCUSE IN HISTORY FOR HOW THE GOLDEN CALF CAME ABOUT.

Exodus 32:24—And I said unto them, Whosoever hath any gold, let them break it off. So they gave it me: then I cast it into the fire, and there came out this calf.

## THE LORD'S RULES REGARDING LEFTOVERS.

Leviticus 19:6—It shall be eaten the same day ye offer it, and on the morrow: and if ought remain until the third day, it shall be burnt in the fire.

## SELLING DEAD MEAT TO ALIENS?

Deuteronomy 14:21—Ye shall not eat of any thing that dieth of itself: thou shalt give it unto the stranger that is in thy gates, that he may eat it; or thou mayest sell it unto an alien.

## YEARLONG HONEYMOONS REQUIRED!

Deuteronomy 24:5—When a man hath taken a new wife, he shall not go out to war, neither shall he be charged with any business: but he shall be free at home one year, and shall cheer up his wife which he hath taken.

## WHAT THE KIDS NAMED THE ALTAR.

Joshua 22:34—And the children of Reuben and the children of Gad called the altar Ed.

## WHAT HAPPENS IF YOU STAB SOMEONE TOO DEEPLY?

Judges 3:21–22—And Ehud put forth his left hand, and took the dagger from his right thigh, and thrust it into his belly: And the haft [or handle] also went in after the blade; and the fat closed upon the blade, so that he could not draw the dagger out of his belly; and the dirt came out.

## BE SURE TO GIVE HIM ONE OF YOUR SHOES TO SEAL THE DEAL.

Ruth 4:7–8—To confirm all things; a man plucked off his shoe, and gave it to his neighbour: and this was a testimony in Israel. Therefore the kinsman said unto Boaz, Buy it for thee. So he drew off his shoe.

## ELIJAH HAVING FUN WITH THE PRIESTS OF BAAL, WHO PRAYED IN VAIN FOR THEIR IDOL TO LIGHT THEIR SACRIFICE.

1 Kings 18:27—And it came to pass at noon, that Elijah mocked them, and said, Cry aloud: for he is a god; either he is talking, or he is pursuing, or he is in a journey, or peradventure he sleepeth, and must be awaked.

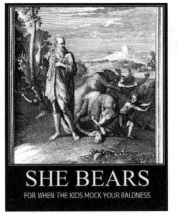

SHE BEARS
FOR WHEN THE KIDS MOCK YOUR BALDNESS

## KIDS, PLEASE DON'T TEASE THE PROPHET ELISHA ABOUT HIS BALDNESS!

2 Kings 2:23–24—And he went up from thence unto Beth-el: and as he was going up by the way, there came forth little children out of the city, and mocked him, and said unto him, Go up, thou bald head; go up, thou bald head.

And he turned back, and looked on them, and cursed them in the name of the Lord. And there came forth two she bears out of the wood, and tare forty and two children of them.

**"A MERRY HEART DOETH GOOD LIKE A MEDICINE."**
**PROVERB 17:22**

## CAB DRIVERS IN THE BIBLE?

2 Kings 9:20—And the watchman told, saying, He came even unto them, and cometh not again: and the driving is like the driving of Jehu the son of Nimshi; for he driveth furiously.

## YES, MEN CAN DO THE DISHES!

2 Kings 21:13—I will wipe Jerusalem as a man wipeth a dish, wiping it, and turning it upside down.

## "BY THE POWER OF GRAYSKULL!" HE-MAN IN THE BIBLE.

1 Chronicles 25:5—All these were the sons of Heman the king's seer in the words of God, to lift up the horn. And God gave to Heman fourteen sons and three daughters.

## GOOD VERSE TO SHARE WITH YOUR TEENAGERS ON A SATURDAY MORNING.

Proverb 6:9—How long wilt thou sleep, O sluggard? When wilt thou arise out of thy sleep?

## WEIGHT PROBLEMS FOR DEMOCRATS?

Proverb 11:25—The liberal soul shall be made fat.

## I DON'T CARE IF YOU ARE BLESSING ME OR CURSING ME, BUT KEEP IT DOWN IN THE MORNING, NEIGHBOR!

Proverb 27:14—He that blesseth his friend with a loud voice, rising early in the morning, it shall be counted a curse to him.

## DEEP THOUGHTS ABOUT CAUSE AND EFFECT.

Proverb 30:33—Surely the churning of milk bringeth forth butter, and the wringing of the nose bringeth forth blood: so the forcing of wrath bringeth forth strife.

## DOES NIXON KNOW ABOUT THIS BREAK-IN?

Nehemiah 8:1—And all the people gathered themselves together as one man into the street that was before the water gate.

## SOMETIMES IT IS WISER TO KEEP YOUR MOUTH SHUT!

Job 13:5—O that ye would altogether hold your peace! and it should be your wisdom.

## PEANUT BUTTER IN OLD TESTAMENT TIMES?

Job 29:10—The nobles held their peace, and their tongue cleaved to the roof of their mouth.

## WHAT HAPPENED TO THE STORMTROOPERS IN THEIR BATTLE WITH THE EWOKS?

Psalms 83:10—Which perished at En-dor: they became as dung for the earth.

## STAY CLEAR OF THOSE BRAWLING WOMEN!

Proverb 21:9—It is better to dwell in a corner of the housetop, than with a brawling woman in a wide house.

## NBA PLAYERS CAN EMPATHIZE WITH THIS.

Isaiah 28:20—For the bed is shorter than that a man can stretch himself on it: and the covering narrower than that he can wrap himself in it.

## A WARNING TO KATNISS EVERDEEN—"GIRL ON FIRE"—OF HUNGER GAMES FAME.

Isaiah 50:11—Behold all ye that kindle a fire, that compass yourselves about with sparks: walk in the light of your fire, and in the sparks that ye have kindled. This shall ye have of mine hand; ye shall lie down in sorrow.

## AM I SUPPOSED TO STAND UP OR SIT? SO CONFUSED!

Isaiah 52:2—Shake thyself from the dust; arise, sit down, O Jerusalem.

## HOW SOME ELDERS IN THE MTC FEEL AFTER EXTRA HEAVY MEALS.

Jeremiah 4:19—My bowels, my bowels! I am pained at my very heart; my heart maketh a noise in me; I cannot hold my peace, because thou hast heard, O my soul, the sound of the trumpet, the alarm of war.

## CHRISTMAS TREES IN OLD TESTAMENT TIMES?

Jeremiah 10:3–4—For the customs of the people are vain: for one cutteth a tree out of the forest, the work of the hands of the workman, with the axe. They deck it with silver and with gold.

## COOKING THAT'S A LITTLE TOO ORGANIC FOR ME!

Ezekiel 4:12—And thou shalt eat it as barley cakes, and thou shalt bake it with dung that cometh out of man, in their sight.

## WHAT TO SAY WHEN YOU MEET SOME NICE WHEELS.

Ezekiel 10:13—As for the wheels, it was cried unto them in my hearing, O wheel.

## SCRIPTURAL EVIDENCE OF SANTA CLAUS!

Zechariah 2:6—Ho, ho, come forth, and flee from the land of the north, saith the Lord: for I have spread you abroad as the four winds of the heaven.

## BIBLICAL RECORD OF THE FIRST FOOD FIGHT (OR MAYBE THE FIRST TOILET-PAPERING INCIDENT).

Zechariah 5:1–2—Then I turned, and lifted up mine eyes, and looked, and behold a flying roll. And he said unto me, What seest thou? And I answered, I see a flying roll; the length thereof is twenty cubits, and the breadth thereof ten cubits.

## WHAT HAPPENS IN CITIES WITHOUT PARKS AND PLAYGROUNDS?

Zechariah 8:5—And the streets of the city shall be full of boys and girls playing in the streets thereof.

The New Testament, though not as arcane as the Old, still has some zingers. Unfortunately, a few are a bit of a stretch and may elicit more groans than laughs. But bear with me and have some fun anyway.

## DID JOSEPH AND MARY HAVE A PET FLEA?

Matthew 2:13—And when they were departed, behold, the angel of the Lord appeareth to Joseph in a dream, saying, Arise, and take the young child and his mother, and flee into Egypt.

### HUMOR IS APPROPRIATE

"WE'VE GOT TO HAVE A LITTLE HUMOR IN OUR LIVES. YOU HAD BETTER TAKE SERIOUSLY THAT WHICH SHOULD BE TAKEN SERIOUSLY BUT, AT THE SAME TIME, WE CAN BRING IN A TOUCH OF HUMOR NOW AND AGAIN. IF THE TIME EVER COMES WHEN WE CAN'T SMILE AT OURSELVES, IT WILL BE A SAD TIME."‡

‡Gordon B. Hinckley, *Teachings of Gordon B. Hinckley* (Salt Lake City: Deseret Book, 1997), 432.

## DOES THE NEW TESTAMENT PROHIBIT TELEVISION?

Matthew 17:9—And as they came down from the mountain, Jesus charged them, saying, Tell the vision to no man.

## MATTHEW GIVES US AN EMOTICON SMILE :)

Matthew 24:15—When ye therefore shall see the abomination of desolation, spoken of by Daniel the prophet, stand in the holy place, (whoso readeth, let him understand:).

## STREAKING IN THE BIBLE?

Mark 14:52—And he left the linen cloth, and fled from them naked.

## HOW DID ALL THREE FIT IN ONE SMALL MANGER?

Luke 2:16—And they came with haste, and found Mary, and Joseph, and the babe lying in a manger.

## LUKE TALKING ABOUT TATOOINE?

Luke 9:12—For we are here in a desert place.

## JESUS IS SO FED UP WITH HEROD, HE CALLS HIM A FOX!

Luke 13:32—And he said unto them, Go ye, and tell that fox, Behold, I cast out devils, and I do cures to day and to morrow, and the third day I shall be perfected.

## EXCUSE FOR WHY YOU CAN'T GO ON THE GUYS' WEEKEND TO VEGAS.

Luke 14:20—And another said, I have married a wife, and therefore I cannot come.

## JESUS'S FAVORITE BREAKFAST CEREAL IS REVEALED.

Luke 24:42—And they gave him a piece of a broiled fish, and of an honeycomb.

## PROPHECY OF THE MODERN U.S. CONGRESS.

Acts 19:32—Some therefore cried one thing, and some another: for the assembly was confused; and the more part knew not wherefore they were come together.

## WAS THE APOSTLE PAUL A HIGH COUNCIL SPEAKER?

Acts 20:9—And there sat in a window a certain young man named Eutychus, being fallen into a deep sleep: and as Paul was long preaching, he sunk down with sleep, and fell down from the third loft, and was taken up dead. (Don't worry. Paul raises Eutychus from the dead later in the chapter.)

## SAFEST WAY TO DEAL WITH YOUR MISSION COMPANION'S COOKING.

Colossians 2:21—Touch not; taste not; handle not.

## PAUL GIVES US A WINK ;)

Colossians 2:22—Which all are to perish with the using;)

## HOW TO MORTIFY THE MEMBERS!

Colossians 3:5—Mortify therefore your members which are upon the earth; fornication, uncleanness, inordinate affection, evil concupiscence, and covetousness, which is idolatry.

## DON'T CONFUSE JOHN AND 1 JOHN IN THE NEW TESTAMENT!

To calm her nerves, an anxious bride insisted to the wedding planner that her favorite verse be written on her wedding cake: 1 John 4:18

"There is no fear in love; but perfect love casteth out fear."

A few days before her wedding day, the bride received a call from the caterer, who asked, "Is this really the verse you want on your cake?"

"Of course!" she insisted.

It was a beautiful wedding day, and the bride thought everything was perfect—until she saw the cake at the reception. The words decorated so beautifully on the cake read: "For thou hast had five husbands; and he whom thou now hast is not thy husband" (John 4:18).

## PROOF THAT CHATTERBOXES WON'T MAKE IT TO HEAVEN.

Revelation 8:1—And when he had opened the seventh seal, there was silence in heaven about the space of half an hour.

And yes, fun verses do exist outside of the Bible. See if any of these verses from the Book of Mormon and Doctrine and Covenants get you to smile.

## GREAT EXCUSE TO AVOID THAT DIET.

2 Nephi 9:51—Feast upon that which perisheth not, neither can be corrupted, and let your soul delight in fatness.

## DOH! ABINADI BLOWS HIS OWN COVER.

Mosiah 12:1—And it came to pass that after the space of two years that Abinadi came among them in disguise, that they knew him not, and began to prophesy among them, saying: Thus has the Lord commanded me, saying—Abinadi, go and prophesy unto this my people. . . .

## HARSH PROPHECY BY ABINADI.

Mosiah 12:5—Yea, and I will cause that they shall have burdens lashed upon their backs; and they shall be driven before like a dumb ass.

## HANDY VERSE TO SHARE IF YOUR DATE GETS TOO FRISKY.

Mosiah 13:3—Touch me not, for God shall smite you if ye lay your hands upon me.

## NEVER MIX UP 3 NEPHI WITH 1 NEPHI.

A senior missionary asked his brand new companion to share his favorite scripture when they were teaching

ONCE AN UPSET WOMAN CAME TO BRIGHAM YOUNG FOR ADVICE AND EXPLAINED TO HIM, "MY HUSBAND JUST TOLD ME TO GO TO HELL. WHAT SHOULD I DO?" PRESIDENT YOUNG SIMPLY REPLIED, "DON'T GO."‡

‡ Stephanie Rhodes, "A Time to Laugh: The Place of Humor in the Church," *The Digital Universe*, Aug. 16, 2011, http://universe.byu.edu/2011/08/16/a-time-to-laugh-the-place-of-humor-in-the-church/.

a young man investigating the gospel. A little bit nervous and with his foreign language skills a little underdeveloped, the greenie accidentally directed the investigator to read 3 Nephi 3:7 aloud.

The elders were waiting to hear the classic words of 1 Nephi 3:7—"I will go and do the things which the Lord hath commanded"—but imagine their wide eyes when the young man read, "Or in other words, yield yourselves up unto us, and unite with us and become acquainted with our secret works, and become our brethren that ye may be like unto us—not our slaves, but our brethren and partners of all our substance."

## SOOOO GLAD GOVERNOR LACHONEUS DIDN'T MAKE THE NEPHITES ALSO GATHER ALL THEIR LAND IN ONE PLACE. CAN YOU IMAGINE?

3 Nephi 3:13—Yea, he sent a proclamation among all the people, that they should gather together their women, and their children, their flocks and their herds, and all their substance, save it were their land, unto one place.

## ALL DOGS DON'T GO TO HEAVEN!

Moroni 10:33—That ye become holy, without spot.

## IS SATAN REALLY A PROMISCUOUS WOMAN?

Doctrine and Covenants 52:14—And again, I will give unto you a pattern in all things, that ye may not be deceived; for Satan is abroad in the land.

## A POOR CHOICE OF SCRIPTURE TO SHARE BEFORE INTRODUCING YOUR FEATURED SPEAKER.

Doctrine and Covenants 84:70—And the tongue of the dumb shall speak.

So, guys, stay awake during scripture study. You never know when the Lord will test your sense of humor. By not alertly looking at each passage of scripture, you may miss wording that will make you smile.

# Six

# LEGENDARY BATTLES

The Bible and Book of Mormon are filled with battles—Nephites versus Lamanites, Israelites versus Philistines, and many more. Some are notable for their strangeness, like when Samson defeats 1,000 Philistines using the jawbone of an ass (see Judges 15:15); others for dramatic moments, like Captain Moroni's guard scalping Zerahemnah (see Alma 44:13); and still others are memorable because miracles ended them before they really started—think David defeating Goliath and sending the Philistines running (see 1 Samuel 17) or Joshua's priests circling the walls of Jericho and then seeing them crumble (see Joshua 6).

But among all of the battles in the scriptures, let's take a look at the five bloodiest.

## FINAL JAREDITE BATTLE (2,000,000+ SLAIN)

The final Jaredite battle between the forces of Shiz and Coriantumr is far and away the bloodiest battle in all of scripture—"There had been slain two millions of mighty men, and also their wives and their children" (Ether 15:2). It is true that this number probably represents all who died in the war up to that point and not just in the final specific battle, per se, but this is still a higher death toll than every other battle in the scriptures *combined*. This is *nine times worse* than

the final Nephite-Lamanite struggle at Cumorah. This is worse than the 1.2 million dead at the Battle of the Somme, the bloodiest battle in World War I, and worse than the 1.3 million American military and civilian dead from every single U.S. conflict since 1775 *combined*. There have been battles with higher death tolls in history but very, very few.

Scholar Hugh Nibley notes:

> The insane wars of the Jaredite chiefs ended in the complete annihilation of both sides, with the kings the last to go. This all seems improbable to us, but two circumstances peculiar to Asiatic warfare explain why the phenomenon is by no means without parallel: (1) Since every war is strictly a personal contest between kings, the battle *must* continue until one of the kings falls or is taken. (2) And yet things are so arranged that the king must be very *last* to fall, the whole army existing for the sole purpose of defending his person. This is clearly seen in the game of chess, in which all pieces are expendable except the king. . . . So let no one think the final chapter of Ether is at all fanciful or overdrawn. Wars of extermination are a standard institution in the history of Asia.[40]

Sometime around 200 B.C., there were various plots and schemes to dethrone King Coriantumr of the Jaredites. A rival named Shared actually captured the king at one point, but the king's sons freed him. "Now there began to be a war upon all the face of the land, every man with his band fighting for that which he desired" (Ether 13:25).

40 John Welch, Hugh Nibley, Darrell L. Matthews, and Stephen R. Callister, *Lehi in the Desert/The World of the Jaredites/There Were Jaredites* (Salt Lake City: Deseret Book, 1952), 235.

**THE BLOODIEST BATTLE IN HEAVEN** THE WORST SPIRITUAL BATTLE WOULD HAVE BEEN LUCIFER AND HIS FOLLOWERS' REBELLION IN THE PREMORTAL EXISTENCE WHEN THEY DID NOT ACCEPT HEAVENLY FATHER'S PLAN AND JEHOVAH'S ROLE IN IT: "AND THERE WAS WAR IN HEAVEN: MICHAEL AND HIS ANGELS FOUGHT AGAINST THE DRAGON; AND THE DRAGON FOUGHT AND HIS ANGELS, AND PREVAILED NOT; NEITHER WAS THEIR PLACE FOUND ANY MORE IN HEAVEN. AND THE GREAT DRAGON WAS CAST OUT, THAT OLD SERPENT, CALLED THE DEVIL, AND SATAN, WHICH DECEIVETH THE WHOLE WORLD: HE WAS CAST OUT INTO THE EARTH, AND HIS ANGELS WERE CAST OUT WITH HIM" (REVELATION 12:7–9). SO WHAT WAS THE CASUALTY COUNT ON THIS ONE? WE KNOW "A THIRD PART OF THE HOSTS OF HEAVEN" WAS CAST OUT (D&C 29:36). HOWEVER, WE DO NOT KNOW IF THAT MEANS ONE-THIRD OF THE TENS OF BILLIONS OF SPIRIT CHILDREN OR IF IT JUST MEANS A THIRD GROUP (WITH THE "NOBLE AND GREAT ONES" AS THE FIRST GROUP AND THE OTHERS WHO FOLLOWED GOD'S PLAN AS THE SECOND GROUP). EITHER WAY, IT COULD HAVE BEEN BILLIONS OF LOST SOULS!

Coriantumr eventually defeated Shared and battled with the forces of Shared's brother Gilead. But just as Gilead was gaining power in the land, he was betrayed by a man named Lib, who also fought it out with Coriantumr for a while. Ultimately, Coriantumr defeated and killed Lib. But Lib's brother Shiz picked up where Lib left off, and this was what led to the great final Jaredite battle: Shiz versus Coriantumr.

Shiz goes on a rampage in his pursuit of Coriantumr: "And it came to pass that Shiz pursued after Coriantumr, and he did overthrow many cities, and he did slay both women and children, and he did burn the cities. And there went a fear of Shiz throughout all the land; yea, a cry went forth throughout the land—Who can stand before the army of Shiz? Behold, he sweepeth the earth before him!" (Ether 14:17–18). The destruction and the horror were so great that everyone chose a side— the conquering Shiz or the defending Coriantumr. And things got bad:

And so great and lasting had been the war, and so long had been the scene of bloodshed and carnage, that the whole face of the land was covered with the bodies of the dead.

And so swift and speedy was the war that there was none left to bury the dead, but they did march forth from the shedding of blood to the shedding of blood, leaving the bodies of both men, women, and children strewed upon the face of the land, to become a prey to the worms of the flesh.

And the scent thereof went forth upon the face of the land, even upon all the face of the land; wherefore the people became troubled by day and by night, because of the scent thereof.

Nevertheless, Shiz did not cease to pursue Coriantumr; for he had sworn to avenge himself upon Coriantumr of the blood of his brother, who had been slain. (Ether 14:21–24)

Shiz's armies drove Coriantumr's forces eastward to the seashore, where they fought for three days. New recruits of Shiz—realizing it was better to join his side than oppose him—gathered together in the valley of Corihor. Coriantumr's army regrouped and pitched their

**"GENERAL" AUTHORITIES** WHEN JOSEPH SMITH ORGANIZED THE NAUVOO LEGION, HE GAVE HIMSELF THE RANK OF LIEUTENANT GENERAL AND BECOME ITS LEADER. THIS RILED SOME NON-MORMONS BECAUSE THE ONLY AMERICAN WHO HAD HELD THE HIGH RANK OF LIEUTENANT GENERAL TO THAT POINT WAS GEORGE WASHINGTON IN THE REVOLUTIONARY WAR! LATER, THE TITLE WAS GIVEN TO WINFIELD SCOTT IN THE MEXICAN WAR AND ULYSSES S. GRANT IN THE CIVIL WAR, AND BECAME MORE FREQUENTLY USED IN LATER AMERICAN HISTORY.

BUT SPEAKING OF GENERALS, BESIDES JOSEPH SMITH, TWO OTHER MILITARY GENERALS HAVE SERVED AS LDS GENERAL AUTHORITIES. JOHN R. LASATER, A RETIRED U.S. AIR FORCE BRIGADIER GENERAL, SERVED AS A MEMBER OF BOTH THE FIRST QUORUM OF THE SEVENTY AND THE SECOND QUORUM OF THE SEVENTY BETWEEN 1987 AND 1992. ROBERT C. OAKS WAS THE FIRST LDS FOUR-STAR GENERAL, WAS THE HEAD OF THE AIR TRAINING COMMAND, AND WAS COMMANDER OF THE UNITED STATES AIR FORCE IN EUROPE. HE SERVED IN THE SECOND QUORUM OF THE SEVENTY AND THE PRESIDENCY OF THE SEVENTY FROM 2000 TO 2009.

tents in the valley of Shurr at the base of the hill Comnor. When they were ready for the next assault, "Coriantumr did gather his armies together upon the hill Comnor, and did sound a trumpet unto the armies of Shiz to invite them forth to battle" (Ether 14:28).

Shiz's army came forward, and while Shiz's army was likely larger in numbers than that of their opponents, Coriantumr had the advantage of the high ground. Shiz's forces were driven back twice, but on their third attempt up the hill Comnor, they broke through. Shiz himself inflicted such great wounds on Coriantumr that Coriantumr fainted for loss of blood and had to be hauled away by his men. "Now the loss of men, women and children on both sides was so great that Shiz commanded his people that they should not pursue the armies of Coriantumr; wherefore, they returned to their camp" (Ether 14:31).

It was while recovering from his wounds that King Coriantumr took inventory of the carnage and learned that the death toll to that point had reached 2,000,000. Coriantumr tried to broker a peace with Shiz but to no avail. The Jaredite people were so drunk with anger, hate, and revenge that there was no stopping them: "But behold, the Spirit of the Lord had ceased striving with them, and Satan had full power over the hearts of the people; for they were given up unto the hardness of their hearts, and the blindness of their minds that they might be destroyed; wherefore they went again to battle. And it came to pass that they fought all that day, and when the night came they slept upon their swords" (Ether 15:19–20).

After another four years of battle, all the Jaredites were destroyed except Coriantumr, Shiz, who was finally beheaded by Coriantumr, and the prophet Ether, who recorded the horrific scenes from the safety of his cave. Coriantumr ended up stumbling away from this nightmare and being discovered by the Mulekites (see Omni 1:21).

"It is impossible for us to fully fathom the horror of the final Jaredite battle in which even women and children were armed and sent to war," Nibley said. "Here we have a graphic picture of what men

become when the Spirit of the Lord withdraws and no longer strives with them."[41]

## ABIJAH OF JUDAH VERSUS JEROBOAM OF ISRAEL (500,000 SLAIN)

The bloodiest battle of the Bible took place in about 915 B.C. when Abijah, king of Judah, sought to conquer Jeroboam of Israel and reunite the two kingdoms. Abijah was the son of Rehoboam, grandson of Solomon, and great-grandson of David and felt it was his duty as reigning member of the house of David to make Israel whole. He built "an army of valiant men of war," numbering 400,000. In response, Jeroboam built an army of 800,000 "chosen men, being mighty men of valour," to defend the sovereignty of the rebellious northern kingdom.

The conflict began at the border of the Northern Kingdom of Israel and the Southern Kingdom of Judah in the densely wooded mountain district of central Palestine called the mountains of Ephraim. Abijah stood atop Mount Zemaraim in that range and cried to the assembled foes:

> Ought ye not to know that the Lord God of Israel gave the kingdom over Israel to David for ever, even to him and to his sons by a covenant of salt?

> Yet Jeroboam the son of Nebat, the servant of Solomon the son of David, is risen up, and hath rebelled against his lord. . . .

---

41 *Book of Mormon Student Manual* (Salt Lake City: The Church of Jesus Christ of Latter-day Saints, 1996), http://www.ldsces.org/manuals/book-of-mormon-insti-tute-student-manual/bm1996-09-mor-9-5.asp.

And now ye think to withstand the kingdom of the Lord in the hand of the sons of David; and ye be a great multitude, and there are with you golden calves, which Jeroboam made you for gods. . . .

But as for us, the Lord is our God, and we have not forsaken him. . . .

And, behold, God himself is with us for our captain, and his priests with sounding trumpets to cry alarm against you. O children of Israel, fight ye not against the Lord God of your fathers; for ye shall not prosper. (2 Chronicles 13:5–12)

The rousing cry for repentance and reunion fell on deaf ears, and the more numerous army of Jeroboam set up an ambush in the dense woods and surprised the army of Judah by attacking from both the front and rear of their formation. Judah had the advantage of the higher ground atop Mount Zemaraim, but Jeroboam had the advantage of having an army twice as large. Jeroboam's advantage was compounded by the element of surprise and opening up a two-front attack.

But Abijah and the armies of Judah had the ultimate advantage of "God as their captain." They prayed aloud to the Lord for help, the priests sounded their trumpets, and then the men of Judah shouted: "And as the men of Judah shouted, it came to pass, that God smote Jeroboam and all Israel before Abijah and Judah. And the children of Israel fled before Judah: and God delivered them into their hand. And Abijah and his people slew them with a great slaughter: so there fell down slain of Israel five hundred thousand chosen men. Thus the children of Israel were brought under at that time, and the children of Judah prevailed, because they relied upon the Lord God of their fathers" (2 Chronicles 13:15–18).

The army of Judah pursued the army of Israel northward, conquering a number of key towns along the borderlands. Jeroboam's forces were crippled and never posed a problem to Israel again, but Abijah did not succeed in uniting the kingdoms in his lifetime. The civil war between

Israel and Judah continued off and on for almost two more centuries. And just as Gettysburg during the Civil War was the bloodiest battle in American history, so was the bloodiest battle in Israel's history its civil war—when Abijah battled Jeroboam in the mountains of Ephraim. But the mountains where righteous Judah secured this miraculous victory still, to this day, represent a place of divine protection and deliverance, as we sing in the hymn: "O Babylon, O Babylon, we bid thee farewell; / We're going to the mountains of Ephraim to dwell."[42]

# BATTLE OF CUMORAH (230,000 SLAIN)

Perhaps the most famous battle in the Book of

**TWO CUMORAHS? MORONI EVENTUALLY BURIES THE GOLD PLATES IN A HILL IN MODERN-DAY NEW YORK STATE, WHICH LATTER-DAY SAINTS CALL CUMORAH. IN THE BOOK OF MORMON, MORONI NEVER CALLED THE HILL WHERE HE BURIED THE PLATES CUMORAH. THAT NAME IS USED IN THE SCRIPTURES ONLY IN RELATION TO WHERE THE FINAL BATTLE WAS FOUGHT. LDS SCHOLARS AND ARCHAEOLOGISTS CONTINUE TO DEBATE ON WHETHER THE PLATES WERE BURIED IN THE SAME HILL WHERE THE FINAL BATTLE WAS FOUGHT OR WHETHER THERE ARE ACTUALLY TWO CUMORAHS (PERHAPS THE BATTLE CUMORAH IS IN MESOAMERICA). THE CHURCH IS OFFICIALLY NEUTRAL ON THIS AS WELL AS ON ALL QUESTIONS PERTAINING TO BOOK OF MORMON GEOGRAPHY.‡**

Mormon is the final Nephite and Lamanite conflict. Off and on since he was age 16, the mighty Nephite prophet-general Mormon led his people in their struggles against the Lamanites. By AD 384, Mormon knew it was time for a final showdown to see if the Nephites could

---

42 *Hymns*, no. 319.

‡ Correspondence from F. Michael Watson, Office of the First Presidency, 23 April 1993, as cited in William J. Hamblin, "Basic Methodological Problems with the Anti-Mormon Approach to the Geography and Archaeology of the Book of Mormon," *Journal of Book of Mormon Studies* 2/1 (1993): 181; see also Daniel H. Ludlow, ed., *Encyclopedia of Mormonism*, 1992, 346.

begin to turn the tide on the destruction the Lamanites continued to wreak on them.

Mormon sent an epistle to the king of the Lamanites, telling him he was gathering all the remaining armies in the land of Cumorah and inviting him to come fight them if he dared. "And it came to pass that the king of the Lamanites did grant unto me the thing which I desired," Mormon wrote. So he began marching the Nephites into the land of Cumorah, and Mormon says, "And we did pitch our tents around about the hill Cumorah; and it was in a land of many waters, rivers, and fountains; and here we had hope to gain advantage over the Lamanites" (Mormon 6:3–4). I envision a good game of Stratego, where Mormon uses the water features in the center to strategically defend his army! While they were preparing for the big battle, Mormon hid all of the Nephite records in the hill Cumorah, except for the abridgement on gold plates that he gave his son Moroni.

Can you imagine the fear and dread the Nephite families faced as they pitched their tents in the land of streams and lakes around Cumorah? In addition to the defense the water features provided, they also gave a life source in case the Nephites were trapped in the Cumorah area for a long time, surrounded by Lamanite armies. But such protections were small comfort when they saw the enormous numbers of Lamanites marching toward Cumorah: "And it came to pass that my people, with their wives and their children, did now behold the armies of the Lamanites marching towards them." Mormon wrote, "And with that awful fear of death which fills the breasts of all the wicked, did they await to receive them" (Mormon 6:7).

Mormon organized the remaining Nephite armies into divisions of 10,000. He led his own division, as did his son Moroni. Other leaders of 10,000 soldiers each included Gidgiddonah, Lamah, Gilgal, Limhah, Jeneum, Cumenihah, Moronihah, Antionum, Shiblom, Shem, and Josh. There were also ten other leaders of 10,000, each who are left unnamed, so we know there was a Nephite army of 230,000. But the Lamanite army must have been enormous in comparison: "And it came to pass that they came to battle against us, and every soul was filled with terror because of the greatness of their numbers. And it came to pass that they did fall upon my people with the sword, and with the bow, and with the arrow, and with the ax, and with all manner of weapons of war" (Mormon 6:8–9).

Mormon wrote about fighting alongside his men but watching his entire force get hewn down. Any advantage he had of having the higher ground on the hill Cumorah or using the water in the area as defense was mitigated by the sheer numbers of the Lamanite horde. General Mormon himself was injured and fell to the ground on the hillside among the dead soldiers. Either through divine protection or from the fast-moving Lamanite army simply assuming Mormon was as dead as those he lay among, Mormon wrote that the Lamanites "passed by me that they did not put an end to my life" (Mormon 6:10).

In the morning, after the Lamanites returned to their camps, the few Nephite survivors straggled to the top of the hill Cumorah to survey the decimation. Mormon described the scene: "Their flesh, and bones, and blood lay upon the face of the earth, being left by the hands of those who slew them to molder upon the land, and to crumble and to return to their mother earth" (Mormon 6:15). Only 25 Nephites made it; the rest were dead, had escaped into the south countries, or had deserted and joined the enemy army. Mormon, there with 24 of his colleagues, including his son Moroni, was heartbroken.

> And my soul was rent with anguish, because of the slain of my people, and I cried:
>
> O ye fair ones, how could ye have departed from the ways of the Lord! O ye fair ones, how could ye have rejected that Jesus, who stood with open arms to receive you!
>
> Behold, if ye had not done this, ye would not have fallen. But behold, ye are fallen, and I mourn your loss.
>
> O ye fair sons and daughters, ye fathers and mothers, ye husbands and wives, ye fair ones, how is it that ye could have fallen!

But behold, ye are gone, and my sorrows cannot bring your return. . . .

O that ye had repented before this great destruction had come upon you. But behold, ye are gone, and the Father, yea, the Eternal Father of heaven, knoweth your state; and he doeth with you according to his justice and mercy. (Mormon 6:16–22)

## ANGELIC DEFEAT OF THE ASSYRIANS (185,000 SLAIN)

The fourth bloodiest battle in the scriptures, which occurred in about 700 B.C., is a miraculous account of divine protection. The Assyrians sacked the Northern Kingdom of Israel in 722 B.C., and the ten tribes of that kingdom were relocated or scattered and ultimately became known as the lost ten tribes. Now, Assyria turned their attention to the Southern Kingdom of Judah, home of the remaining two tribes of Judah and Benjamin.

The forces of King Sennacherib of Assyria invaded Judah and captured a number of towns as they approached the capital of Jerusalem. Hezekiah, king of Judah at the time, sent an enormous tribute of gold and silver to the Assyrians, hoping to appease them and keep them away from Jerusalem. But their military leader, Rab-shakeh, pressed on to Jerusalem unsatisfied.

Hezekiah responded to the approaching army by setting "captains of war over the people, and gathered them together to him in the street of the gate of the city." He then, with faith and confidence, attempted to comfort them. "Be strong and courageous, be not afraid nor dismayed for the king of Assyria, nor for all the multitude that is with him," he cried, "for there be more with us than with him: With him is an arm of flesh; but with us is the Lord our God to help us, and to fight our battles. And the people rested themselves upon the words of Hezekiah king of Judah" (2 Chronicles 32:6–8).

In response, Rab-shakeh, the Assyrian general, delivered a blasphemous and vulgar speech in their native Hebrew for all the Jews to hear. He told the noblemen of Judah who were defending the walls of Jerusalem that the king of Assyria had sent him to point out to them that Hezekiah's words of faith were hollow and that if they believed Hezekiah's words, it was as if they were consuming human waste: "Hath he not

sent me to the men which sit on the wall, that they may eat their own dung, and drink their own piss with you?" (2 Kings 18:27). He then mocked the God of Israel and demanded Judah's surrender to Assyria.

"Let not Hezekiah deceive you: for he shall not be able to deliver you out of his hand: Neither let Hezekiah make you trust in the Lord, saying, The Lord will surely deliver us, and this city shall not be delivered into the hand of the king of Assyria," Rab-shakeh said tauntingly at the end of his speech. "Hath any of the gods of the nations delivered at all his land out of the hand of the king of Assyria? . . . Who are they among all the gods of the countries, that have delivered their country out of mine hand, that the Lord should deliver Jerusalem out of mine hand?" (2 Kings 18:30, 33, 35). King Sennacherib himself and his reinforcements, returning from a military campaign in Egypt, further emboldened Rab-shakeh. All the odds were now in favor of an enormous Assyrian victory.

When King Hezekiah heard of the Assyrians at the gates of Jerusalem taunting his people in their own language and threatening to sack the city, he did what any righteous king would do. He sent his chief aides to call on the prophet Isaiah for help and demonstrated humility in the custom of the day by tearing his clothes and going to the temple to pray: "O Lord God of Israel, which dwellest between the cherubims, thou art the God, even thou alone, of all the kingdoms of the earth; thou hast made heaven and earth. Lord, bow down thine ear, and hear: open, Lord, thine eyes, and see: and hear the words of Sennacherib, which hath sent him to reproach the living God. . . .

Now therefore, O Lord our God, I beseech thee, save thou us out of his hand, that all the kingdoms of the earth may know that thou art the Lord God, even thou only" (2 Kings 19:15–16, 19).

King Hezekiah must have been relieved when he returned from the temple and heard Isaiah report the good news: "Thus saith the Lord God of Israel, That which thou hast prayed to me against Sennacherib king of Assyria I have heard. . . . Therefore thus saith the Lord concerning the king of Assyria, He shall not come into this city, nor shoot an arrow there, nor come before it with shield, nor cast a bank against it. By the way that he came, by the same shall he return, and shall not come into this city, saith the Lord. For I will defend this city, to save it, for mine own sake, and for my servant David's sake" (2 Kings 19:20, 32–34).

That night, the angel of the Lord went out among the Assyrian armies camped outside the gates of Jerusalem and "smote in the camp" (2 Kings 19:35), and the angel "cut off all the mighty men of valour, and the leaders and captains in the camp of the king of Assyria" (2 Chronicles 32:21).

And when the Assyrian king awoke early the next morning, he saw he was surrounded by 185,000 corpses—the Assyrian army had been decimated. Jewish tradition holds that it was the angel Gabriel who cursed the Assyrians and that it happened on Passover night with lightning that swept over the enemy camp, causing immediate sickness and death.[43]

43 "2 Chronicles 32: Wesley's Notes on the Bible ," biblehub.com, accessed January 23, 2014, http://biblehub.com/commentaries/wes/2_chronicles/32.htm; See also Louis Ginzberg, Henrietta Szold, Paul Radin, *The Legends of the Jews*, Volume 4: From Joshua to Esther, (Baltimore, MD: Johns Hopkins University Press, 1913), 268.

Regardless of the angel's method, Sennacherib took the survivors and retreated back to the Assyrian capital of Nineveh, never to return to Judah again. "Thus the Lord saved Hezekiah and the inhabitants of Jerusalem from the hand of Sennacherib the king of Assyria, and from the hand of all other, and guided them on every side" (2 Chronicles 32:22).

## PEKAH'S INVASION OF JUDAH (120,000 SLAIN)

Despite King Hezekiah of Judah's righteous leadership, his father, King Ahaz, was idolatrous and wicked and suffered the opposite fate of his son. While Hezekiah was protected from his enemies because of his faith in the Lord, Ahaz suffered a great defeat because of his apostasy—so great that it ranks as the fifth bloodiest battle in scripture.

Ahaz was age 20 when he began his reign and got caught up in the idolatry of the era, building altars and offering sacrifices and incense to Baalim. He defiled the temple and took the "molten sea" (or font) off the backs of the twelve oxen. And in his wickedness, he even sacrificed one of his sons. His wickedness affected Judah, who suffered greatly because of his father's actions: "For the Lord brought Judah low because of Ahaz king of Israel; for he made Judah naked, and transgressed sore against the Lord" (2 Chronicles 28:19).

In 732 B.C., Pekah, king of the Northern Kingdom o f Israel, allied with Rezin, the king of Aram out of Damascus, and invaded Judah. They captured a "great multitude" of Jews and relocated them to Damascus, and Ahaz's forces were "also delivered into the hand of the king of Israel, who smote him with a great slaughter." But how bad was the slaughter of the Jewish army? "For Pekah the son of Remaliah slew in Judah an hundred and twenty thousand in one day, which were all valiant men; because they had forsaken the Lord God of their fathers" (2 Chronicles 28:5–6).

**HOW MANY MORMONS DIED IN WORLD WAR II?** WITH AN ESTIMATED **50 TO 85** MILLION FATALITIES, THE SECOND WORLD WAR WAS BY FAR THE DEADLIEST CONFLICT IN HUMAN HISTORY. "THE FIRST RECORDED DEATHS OF LATTER-DAY SAINT SOLDIERS WERE GERMAN SOLDIERS WHO WERE KILLED JUST DAYS AFTER THE GERMAN INVASION OF POLAND," ROBERT C. FREEMAN, DIRECTOR OF THE SAINTS AT WAR PROJECT, BRIGHAM YOUNG UNIVERSITY, SAID, "BY THE END OF THE WAR, APPROXIMATELY **5,000** LATTER-DAY SAINT SERVICEMEN FROM ALLIED AND AXIS NATIONS HAD DIED."‡

Judah was severely weakened. To lose 120,000 in *one* day is a massive blow. It was more than twice the casualties of Gettysburg, and that horrific Civil War battle occurred over three days. One of the Israeli heroes of the battle was Zichri, "a mighty man of Ephraim," who killed Prince Maaseiah, King Ahaz's son, as well as Azrikam, who was the governor of Ahaz's palace, and King Ahaz's chief advisor Elkanah. In addition to the 120,000 dead, the Israeli army captured 200,000 Jewish women and children and took them and great spoils of war north to their stronghold in Samaria.

It is fascinating to compare righteous Hezekiah's response to invasion to his wicked father's. While Hezekiah turned to the prophet, prayer, and the temple, Ahaz "took the silver and gold that was found in the house of the Lord, and in the treasures of the king's house, and sent it for a present to the king of Assyria" (2 Kings 16:8). He sent the valuables of the temple to Tilgath-pilneser of Assyria, begging him for help. "And Tilgath-pilneser king of Assyria came unto him, and distressed him, but strengthened him not" (2 Chronicles 28:20).

Judah suffered further weakening under the reign of idolatrous Ahaz. The Philistines attacked from the east, carrying off prisoners and treasure. The Edomites attacked from the west, destroying Jewish towns. And when Ahaz died at the end of his sixteen-year reign, the people were so disgusted that "they brought him not into the

---

‡ Robert C. Freeman, "Remembering World War II: Pearl Harbor and Beyond," http://lib.byu.edu/exhibits/wwii/essay.html.

sepulchres of the kings of Israel," and he was buried elsewhere in Jerusalem (2 Chronicles 28:27). It would be up to his righteous son Zedekiah to return Judah to Jehovah and strengthen its military position in the region.

## Seven
# TALLEST, OLDEST, WISEST, AND MORE

In the spirit of popular books of world records or believe-it-or-not listings, let's take a look at the tallest, the oldest, the wisest, and other record-setting facts of the scriptures.

## TALLEST

If you ask someone who the tallest person in the scriptures is, they will likely instinctively answer "Goliath!" After all, the 6.5 cubits of Goliath of Gath are famous (putting him at 9 feet 7 inches). But while the most famous of the Bible's giants, he was certainly not the only one, nor was he the tallest.

Goliath had a few siblings mentioned in the Bible, all children of Raphah of Gath, including one "man of great stature, that had on every hand six fingers, and on every foot six toes, four and twenty in number; and he also was born to the giant" (2 Samuel 21:20). Though we don't know his exact height, to put this in perspective using characters from *The Princess Bride*, Goliath's brother had the stature of Fezzik and the six-fingered hands of Count Rugen. Inigo Montoya may have struggled to avenge his father's death against such a man!

There were giants before the Flood: "There were giants in the earth in those days," and we read about their intermingling with the children of God, which produced "mighty men . . . men of renown" (Genesis 6:4). Giants even tried to kill the prophet Noah: "And in those days there were giants on the earth, and they sought Noah to take away his life; but the Lord was with Noah, and the power of the Lord was upon him" (Moses 8:18).

The first Israelite spies were astonished at some of the giants they discovered in Palestine: "And there we saw the giants, the sons of Anak, which come of the giants: and we were in our own sight as grasshoppers, and so we were in their sight" (Numbers 13:33). The Hebrews called this race of giants Anakims, the Moabites called them Emims, and the Ammonites called them Zamzummims (see Deuteronomy 2:11, 20).

Moses was apparently not afraid of these reports, and he smote and cast out most of the giants from around the edges of the promised land (see Joshua 13:12). We always think of David fighting giants, but we forget that both Noah and Moses were prophets who waged battles with them too.

As Moses and his army were going along conquering towns and slaying giants, they came upon the greatest one of all: "Then we turned, and went up the way to Bashan: and Og the king of Bashan came out against us, he and all his people, to battle at Edrei" (Deuteronomy 3:1). King Og of Bashan was not only the greatest of the giants but was the tallest person mentioned in the scriptures. His bed of iron was described as nine cubits long (13 feet 3 inches) and four cubits wide (5 feet 11 inches) (see Deuteronomy 3:11).

Even if King Og was a full cubit shorter than his bed length, it put t h e

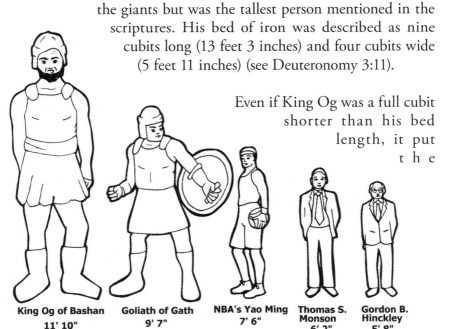

**King Og of Bashan**  **Goliath of Gath**  **NBA's Yao Ming**  **Thomas S.**  **Gordon B.**
**11' 10"**            **9' 7"**           **7' 6"**          **Monson**    **Hinckley**
                                                                **6' 2"**     **5' 8"**

guy at a whopping 11 feet 10 inches tall. This is one-third taller than the tallest man in modern times, the 8-foot 11-inch Giant of Illinois, Robert Wadlow. If King Og played basketball, he would have had to *look down* to put the ball in the 10-foot-tall hoop. Amos described him as a man "whose height was like the height of the cedars, and he was strong as the oaks" (Amos 2:9).

Moses recorded the divine help in defeating this king of giants: "And the Lord said unto me, Fear him not: for I will deliver him, and all his people, and his land, into thy hand. . . . So the Lord our God delivered into our hands Og also, the king of Bashan, and all his people: and we smote him until none was left to him remaining" (Deuteronomy 3:2–4). Centuries later when David wrote the Psalms—himself a giant slayer—he twice celebrated Israel's victory over Og of Bashan, the tallest and most formidable physical presence in the scriptures (see Psalms 135:11 and 136:20).

## OLDEST

The oldest person in the scriptures is Methuselah, who reached 969 years of age. Second oldest is his grandfather Jared, who died at the ripe old age of 962, with third place going to the first man, Adam, who departed at age 930. These ages seem truly unbelievable when we consider that the oldest person in modern times was Jeanne Calment of France, who died in 1997 at the age of 122 ½.

So how did these ancient patriarchs live so long? The short answer is, we don't know, but there are plenty of wild guesses! Some speculate that as we got genetically farther from our perfect parents in the Garden of Eden, human frailties and defects emerged to bring us down to the ages we call "average" today. Man was meant to be everlasting, some theorize, and with sin introduced to the world, each generation's life was somewhat shortened. Others wonder if before the Flood, a "vapor canopy" of sorts hung in the firmament, creating a radiation shield in the sky and a wetter, warmer, balmier climate on the earth that somehow allowed longer ages. In the Bible, there is indeed a clear drop-off in ages after the Flood.

Others have speculated that the Fall of Adam led to a literal fall of planet earth from the presence of God, and as our earth careened farther from Kolob in space, it went from that star's reckoning of time to ours. Hence, the amazing ages of the first generations on earth were all relative to the time they were experiencing. When the earth arrived at its current position, these ages leveled out to what we are familiar with today.

Since we believe the Bible to be the word of God only "as far as it is translated correctly" (Article of Faith 1:8), some believe these ancient ages must simply be mistranslations. Some wonder if instead of years the biblical authors meant months. This works in some cases (Methuselah dying at nearly 81 years of age, which is 969 months) but not all (Enoch was 65 when his son Methuselah was born—if that was 65 months, he would have been a five-year-old father). Other scholars believe the big numbers in Genesis were really multiples of ten, so Methuselah would have died at age 96.9.[44]

So we don't really know how to explain these ancient ages, but we do know of plenty of other creations that lived a long time. General Sherman, the largest sequoia tree in the world, is at least 2,200 years old, for example. Some edible ocean clams have been found that have been alive for centuries, including one that was 507 years old. Adwaita was a giant tortoise in India that was born in 1750 and lived to be 256 years old, dying in 2006 in Kolkata's Alipore Zoo. And the oldest living mammal in recent times was a bowhead whale in Alaska that

---

44 For additional theories, see Dr. Bert Thompson, "The Bible, Science, and the Ages of the Patriarchs," *Apologetics Press*, accessed January 23, 2014, https://www. apologeticspress.org/apcontent.aspx?category=11&article=681.

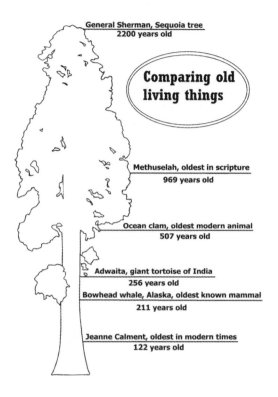

General Sherman, Sequoia tree
2200 years old

**Comparing old living things**

Methuselah, oldest in scripture
969 years old

Ocean clam, oldest modern animal
507 years old

Adwaita, giant tortoise of India
256 years old

Bowhead whale, Alaska, oldest known mammal
211 years old

Jeanne Calment, oldest in modern times
122 years old

experts determined to be 211 years old.[45]

How this longevity really worked out for the biblical patriarchs is definitely a question to ask in the hereafter. Methuselah had quite a life, though, in his 969 years. His father, Enoch, a prophet and the founder of the city of Zion, would have been a solid mentor for the boy Methuselah and "walked with God after he begat Methuselah three hundred years, and begat sons and daughters" (Genesis 5:22).

Methuselah and his siblings would have enjoyed the company of the first man, Adam, and likely his wife, Eve: "Methuselah was one hundred years old when he was ordained under the hand of Adam" (D&C 107:50). Adam would have been 787 years old for the priesthood ordination of his great-great-great-great-great grandson.

When Methuselah was 187, he became the father of Lamech. According to the apocryphal book of Jubilees, Methuselah's wife was named Edna. At age 240, Methuselah was involved in another special event with his prominent forbearer: "Three years previous to the death of Adam, he called Seth, Enos, Cainan, Mahalaleel, Jared, Enoch, and Methuselah, who were all high priests, with the residue of his posterity who were righteous, into the valley of Adam-ondi-Ahman, and there

45 See other examples: "10 Animals That Lived Longer Than the Oldest Known Human," Twisted Sifter, Sep. 19, 2012, http://twistedsifter.com/2012/09/animals-that-lived-longer-than-the-oldest-known-human/.

bestowed upon them his last blessing. And the Lord appeared unto them, and they rose up and blessed Adam, and called him Michael, the prince, the archangel" (D&C 107:53–54).

When Methuselah was 300 years old, Enoch and his city Zion were taken to heaven. Despite being a righteous high priest, Methuselah was not taken to heaven with his father and the other righteous men and women of his generation: "Methuselah, the son of Enoch, was not taken, that the covenants of the Lord might be fulfilled, which he made to Enoch; for he truly covenanted with Enoch that Noah should be of the fruit of his loins" (Moses 8:2).

**HOW FAST CAN YOU RECITE THE BOOKS OF THE BIBLE?** JOSH LEE OF CLINTON, MISSISSIPPI, HOLDS THE CURRENT RECORD OF RECITING ALL **66** BOOKS OF THE BIBLE FROM MEMORY, IN ORDER. HE DID IT IN **22.58** SECONDS ON OCTOBER 19, 2011.[‡] GENESIS, EXODUS, LEVITICUS . . .

And sure enough, when Methuselah was 369, his grandson of prophecy, Noah, was born: "And it came to pass that Methuselah prophesied that from his loins should spring all the kingdoms of the earth (through Noah), and he took glory unto himself" (Moses 8:3). The priesthood was soon passed on to another generation, for "Noah was ten years old when he was ordained under the hand of Methuselah" (D&C 107:52).

The world was getting increasingly wicked in Methuselah's later years. The Apocrypha's book of Jasher tells of Methuselah preaching alongside his grandson Noah to call the world to repentance before the great Flood (see Jasher 5:7). It seems as if the Lord stayed the rains of the Flood until Methuselah died at the age of 969—the very year of the great Flood. Jewish tradition maintains that the rains began to fall just seven days after Methuselah's death.[46]

---

46 The Masoretic Text of Genesis 5.
‡ See "Fastest Time to Recite the 66 Books of the Bible in Order," RecordSetter.com video, accessed January 23, 2014, http://recordsetter.com/world-record/recite-the-66-books-the-bible-order/11385?autoplay=true.

# WISEST

Wisdom is different from intelligence, and being smart is different from being wise. Knowledge is knowing things. Wisdom is knowing how best to apply the things one knows, how to react to situations. Someone could have an amazingly high IQ, like Stephen Hawking's 160, Albert Einstein's 175, chess grandmaster Garry Kasparov's 190, or William James Sidis's world record IQ of 275, but being wise in how that knowledge is used is the key. "Wisdom is the principal thing; therefore get wisdom: and with all thy getting get understanding" (Proverb 4:7).

So who is the wisest in the scriptures? Since there is no "wisdom meter" to measure such a thing, it is not clear cut, but here are a few top contenders.

**Jesus Christ**—It is perhaps obvious that the Son of God tops the list of wisest in the scriptures, since "the Lord by wisdom hath founded the earth" (Proverb 3:19). But His wisdom in mortality did not come all at once. We read of the boy Jesus, "And the child grew, and waxed strong in spirit, filled with wisdom: and the grace of God was upon him" (Luke 2:40). Prophecies foretold of His tremendous wisdom: "And the spirit of the Lord shall rest upon him, the spirit of wisdom and understanding, the spirit of counsel and might, the spirit of knowledge" (Isaiah 11:2).

By the time He began His ministry, no one could question the wisdom of Jesus of Nazareth. He confounded the Pharisees each time they tried to trick Him, He taught gospel principles in brilliant parables the common man could relate with *and* the scholar could find deep meaning in, and He had the highest emotional intelligence, comforting anyone from a woman at a well to a sinner in the street. Jesus spoke of His own wisdom when He referenced the Queen of Sheba, who "came from the uttermost parts of the earth to hear the wisdom of Solomon"; then He declared to the astonished crowd, "And, behold, a greater than Solomon is here" (Matthew 12:42).

**MOST TRAVELED BOOK OF MORMON** A copy of the Book of Mormon taken aboard the Space Shuttle with astronaut Don Lind in April–May 1985 traveled 2,511,592 miles through space as Don orbited the earth 110 times. Don donated these high-flying scriptures to the Church Museum.‡

King Solomon— Certainly the wisest in the Old Testament, Solomon specifically prayed to the Lord for wisdom as a new king and was famously blessed. As we read above, even the Savior Himself referenced Solomon as the high standard of wisdom.

And God gave Solomon wisdom and understanding exceeding much, and largeness of heart, even as the sand that is on the sea shore.

And Solomon's wisdom excelled the wisdom of all the children of the east country, and all the wisdom of Egypt.

For he was wiser than all men; than Ethan the Ezrahite, and Heman, and Chalcol, and Darda, the sons of Mahol: and his fame was in all nations round about.

And he spake three thousand proverbs: and his songs were a thousand and five.

And he spake of trees, from the cedar tree that is in Lebanon even unto the hyssop that springeth out of the wall: he spake also of beasts, and of fowl, and of creeping things, and of fishes.

‡ Skousen, Paul, *The Skousen Book of Mormon World Records* (Springville, Utah: Cedar Fort, Inc., 2004), 151.

And there came of all people to hear the wisdom of Solomon, from all kings of the earth, which had heard of his wisdom. (1 Kings 4:29–34)

**Daniel**—Perhaps more famous in modern times for surviving the lions' den, Daniel also displayed wisdom as a sage advisor to Kings Nebuchadnezzar, Belshazzar, and Darius and became legendary in the ancient world. God gave him "knowledge and skill in all learning and wisdom: and Daniel had understanding in all visions and dreams" (Daniel 1:17). Not only could he interpret dreams, but when asked for advice, he always "answered with counsel and wisdom" (Daniel 2:14). Years later, when the prophet Ezekiel was complimenting the Prince of Tyrus, he referenced the notable wisdom of Daniel: "Behold, thou art wiser than Daniel," he said. "There is no secret that they can hide from thee" (Ezekiel 28:3).

**Wise Men**—When we talk about those with wisdom, we have to include the Wise Men from the East who followed the star and gave gold, frankincense, and myrrh to the infant Jesus. After all, they are not even mentioned in the scriptures by name but instead are simply denoted for their wisdom. They must be wise, right? We are not sure why these gift-givers are called wise men, but we know this much:

1) These were men wise enough to ask for directions when they were lost. In the court of Herod in Jerusalem, they asked, "Where is he that is born King of the Jews? for we have seen his star in the east, and are come to worship him" (Matthew 2:2).

2) These were men wise enough to know to worship Jesus, the son of God: "They saw the young child with Mary his mother, and fell down, and worshipped him" (Matthew 2:11).

3) These were men wise enough to listen and obey God: "And being warned of God in a dream that they should not return to Herod, they departed into their own country another way" (Matthew 2:12).

## STRONGEST

Samson in the Old Testament is well known as the strongest in the scriptures. As a boy, he defeated a lion with his bare hands, and he also broke out of the cords the Philistines bound him with, destroyed a pagan temple with his might, and slew 1,000 men with the jawbone of a donkey (see Judges 14, 15, 16).

## YOUNGEST TO BE ORDAINED

It was pretty remarkable when Noah was ordained to the priesthood at age 10 (see D&C 107:52), but that record fell in New Testament times. In discussing "the lesser priesthood," or Aaronic Priesthood, it was revealed that John the Baptist "was ordained by the angel of God at the time he was eight days old unto this power" (D&C 84:28).

## OLDEST FATHERS

Before the Flood, the oldest father listed was Noah: "And Noah was four hundred and fifty years old, and begat Japheth; and forty-two years afterward he begat Shem of her who was the mother of Japheth, and when he was five hundred years old he begat Ham" (Moses 8:12). After the Flood, the oldest father listed was Abraham: "And Abraham

was an hundred years old, when his son Isaac was born unto him" (Genesis 21:5). In modern times, the oldest father was Les Colley of Australia, who fathered his son Oswald when he was 92 years old. "I never thought she would get pregnant so easy," he said of Oswald's Fijian mother, whom he met through a dating service, "but she . . . did," he told newspaper reporters.[47]

## OLDEST MOTHERS

Presumably, the wives of the antediluvian patriarchs were pretty old when they became mothers. Noah's wife was several hundred years old when Ham was born (Noah was 500 years old). After the flood,

---

47 "Oldest Father," Guinness Book of World Records, accessed January 27, 2014, http://www.guinnessworldrecords.com/world-records/12000/oldest-father-/.

the oldest mother was Sarah, who gave birth to Isaac when she was ninety years old (see Genesis 17:17). When Sarah was promised that she would have a son, "Abraham and Sarah were old and well stricken in age; and it ceased to be with Sarah after the manner of women." Both of them laughed at the idea of conceiving a son at their age, but they were asked, "Is any thing too hard for the Lord?" (Genesis 18:11, 14). And sure enough, Sarah became pregnant at the age of ninety and had a son, whom they named Isaac (Hebrew for "He laugheth"). In modern times, there are nine recorded births to mothers in their seventies, including Mrs. Steve Pace of Rose Hill, Virginia, who in 1939 gave birth to a baby boy at age 73.[48]

## WHICH ARMY HAD 700 LEFT-HANDED MEN?

A special contingent of southpaw sling throwers was an important part of the Benjamanite army: "Among all this people there were seven hundred chosen men lefthanded; every one could sling stones at an hair breadth, and not miss" (Judges 20:16).

## WHOSE HAIR WEIGHED SIX POUNDS WHEN IT WAS CUT ONCE A YEAR?

Absalom was a heartthrob in ancient Israel and only cut his hair once a year. And when he did, it weighed 200 shekels (six pounds): "But in all Israel there was none to be so much praised as Absalom for his beauty: from the sole of his foot even to the crown of his head there was no blemish in him" (2 Samuel 14:25–26). Oh boy.

**WORLD'S LARGEST BIBLE** THE LARGEST BIBLE EVER PRINTED IS A KING JAMES BIBLE CREATED IN 1930 BY A CARPENTER NAMED LOUIS WAYNAI OF LOS ANGELES, CALIFORNIA. USING A LARGE, HOMEMADE, RUBBER-STAMP PRESS, HE PRINTED THE ENORMOUS BOOK, WHICH ENDED UP BEING 43.5 INCHES TALL AND 98 INCHES WIDE, WHEN OPEN. ONCE CLOSED, THE SPINE OF THE BOOK IS 34 INCHES THICK. THE WAYNAI BIBLE WEIGHS 1,094 POUNDS AND CONTAINS 8,048 PAGES.‡

---

48 See "Pregnancy Over Age 50," Wikipedia, accessed January 27, 2014, https://en.wikipedia.org/wiki/Pregnancy_over_age_50.

‡ Info and video online at: "World's Largest Bible," mySavior.info, accessed January 23, 2014, http://mysavior.info/article/394.

## WHO HAD 700 WIVES AND 300 CONCUBINES?

Solomon was supposedly the richest and wisest in the Old Testament, but with 700 wives and 300 concubines to keep track of, I'm beginning to question his wisdom (see 1 Kings 11:3). With this kind of example, it is no wonder that his son Rehoboam "desired many wives." He didn't come close to the size of his dad's harem, but he still had 18 wives and 60 concubines, resulting in 88 children (see 2 Chronicles 11:21, 23). In early Church history, the record for the most wives belongs to Brigham Young, with 55 wives and 57 children. Heber C. Kimball also had an impressive brood, with 43 wives and 65 children.

**LARGEST GROUP TO HOLD A BOOK OF MORMON MARATHON** ON FRIDAY, JAN. 17, 1989, AT 6:00 P.M., A TOTAL OF 224 STUDENTS AT THE GRANGER HIGH SEMINARY IN WEST VALLEY CITY, UTAH, TOOK TURNS READING ALOUD A CHAPTER FROM THE BOOK OF MORMON. THE ALL-NIGHT CHALLENGE CONTINUED UNTIL THEY READ THE LAST CHAPTER IN MORONI AT 3:00 P.M. THE FOLLOWING AFTERNOON.‡

## ANIMALS IN THE SCRIPTURES

Dogs are mentioned 14 times in the Bible and lions 55 times, but domestic cats are not mentioned at all. The raven is the first bird mentioned in the scriptures (see Genesis 8:7). Noah sent it out from the ark to see if the floodwaters had abated, and he also sent the second bird mentioned, a dove, to check the water levels (see Genesis 8:8). Unicorns are mentioned 9 times in the scriptures, but scholars point out that this is a mistranslation of "wild ox" in some verses and "rhinoceros" in others. Dragons are mentioned 48 times in the scriptures and are either symbolic of mythical dragons or mistranslations for animals like jackals and crocodiles.[49] The most mysterious animals in the scriptures are the "cureloms and cumoms" the Jaredites found to be as useful as elephants (Ether 9:19).

## WHO HAD THE NAME MOST LIKELY TO BE TEASED ABOUT ON THE PLAYGROUND?

---

49 For a full list of biblical animals, see "List of Animals in the Bible," Wikipedia, accessed January 27, 2014, https://en.wikipedia.org/wiki/List_of_animals_in_the_Bible#D.

‡ Skousen, Paul, *The Skousen Book of Mormon World Records* (Springville, Utah: Cedar Fort, Inc., 2004), 153.

This is probably a tie between Dodo (see Judges 10:1) and Nimrod (see Genesis 10:8). For the women, it has to be Dorcas (see Acts 9:39).

## WHAT IS THE SHORTEST PRAYER IN SCRIPTURE?

When Peter is sinking while trying to walk on water, he says, "Lord, save me" (Matthew 14:30).

## LONGEST NAME

The longest name in the scriptures tops out at 18 letters for Isaiah's son, Maher-shalal-hash-baz (see Isaiah 8:3). The brother of Jared's true name, Mahonri Moriancumer, is also 18 letters, but Joseph Smith revealed that name to the Cahoon family in Kirtland, Ohio, and it never appeared in the scriptures.

## SHORTEST NAME

Despite being the tallest man in the scriptures, Og, king of Bashan, is one of a handful of people in the scriptures with the shortest name (see Numbers 21:33). Others with two-letter names in the scriptures include Er, the son of Judah (see Numbers 26:19); Ir, father of Shuppim and Huppim (see 1 Chronicles 7:12); So, the king of Egypt (see 2 Kings 17:4); and Uz, grandson of Shem (see Genesis 10:23).

## FIRST NAME ALPHABETICALLY IN THE SCRIPTURES

Aaron is the name that wins this one, and it refers to Aaron, the brother of Moses (see Exodus 4:14); Aaron, the Jaredite king (see Ether 1:16); Aaron, the son of Mosiah (see Mosiah 27:34); and Aaron, king of the Lamanites (see Mormon 2:9).

## LAST NAME ALPHABETICALLY IN THE SCRIPTURES

Zurishaddai, the father of a prince of the children of Simeon, comes last alphabetically in the scriptures (see Numbers 7:36). Zoram, the servant of Laban, who joins Lehi's party, is last alphabetically in the Book of Mormon (see 1 Nephi 4:35). Zoram is also the name of a Nephite chief captain (see Alma 16:5) and a Nephite apostate (see Alma 30:59).

## SHORTEST VERSE
John 11:35—"Jesus wept."

## SECOND SHORTEST VERSE
1 Thessalonians 5:16—"Rejoice evermore."

## OTHER SHORTEST VERSES OUTSIDE OF THE NEW TESTAMENT
Old Testament—1 Chronicles 1:25 "Eber, Peleg, Reu."
Book of Mormon—Alma 18:27 "And he said, Yea."
Doctrine & Covenants 88:36 "All kingdoms have a law given."
Pearl of Great Price—Joseph Smith—Matthew 1:24 "Behold, I have told you before."

## LONGEST VERSES
Pearl of Great Price—Joseph Smith—History 1:28 (211 words, 963 characters).
Doctrine & Covenants 128:18 (209 words, 938 characters).
Book of Mormon—3 Nephi 12:1 (142 words, 598 characters).
New Testament—Revelation 20:4 (67 words, 297 characters).
Old Testament—Esther 8:9 (90 words, 440 characters).

## ON AVERAGE, WHICH BOOK OF SCRIPTURE HAS THE MOST WORDS PER VERSE?
1) Pearl of Great Price—41.54 words.
2) Book of Mormon—40.46 words.
3) Doctrine & Covenants—30.43 words.
4) Old Testament—26.32 words.
5) New Testament—22.67 words.[50]

50 See Laser Jock, "Board Question #37087" Brigham Young University, http://theboard.byu.edu/questions/37087/.

**THE BOOK OF MORMON IN NOTABLE PLACES, WITH NOTABLE PEOPLE** IRENE CORBETT'S COPY OF THE BOOK OF MORMON SANK WITH HER ON THE *TITANIC* IN 1912, AND ONE COPY OF THE BOOK OF MORMON WAS FOUND IN THE RUBBLE OF THE WORLD TRADE CENTER IN 2011. ABRAHAM LINCOLN CHECKED OUT THE BOOK OF MORMON FROM THE LIBRARY OF CONGRESS, AND LORENZO SNOW GAVE A COPY TO QUEEN VICTORIA. POPE JOHN PAUL II WAS GIVEN A BOOK OF MORMON, AND SO WERE MUHAMMAD ALI, ELVIS PRESLEY, SIR WINSTON CHURCHILL, SOVIET PREMIER NIKITA KHRUSHCHEV, QUEEN ELIZABETH II, AND EVERY AMERICAN PRESIDENT SINCE THEODORE ROOSEVELT. NOVELISTS MARK TWAIN AND LEO TOLSTOY EACH HAD A COPY TOO.‡

## SHORTEST CHAPTERS

Psalm 117—33 words in its 2 short verses.
D&C 116—37 words in 1 verse.
Moroni 5—91 words in 2 verses.

## LONGEST CHAPTERS

Psalm 119—176 verses.
Doctrine and Covenants 124—145 verses.
Jacob 5—77 verses.

## SHORTEST BOOK

3 John—14 verses and 299 words.

The following eleven books of scripture also have only one chapter—Obadiah, Jude, Philemon, 2 John, Enos, Jarom, Omni, Words of Mormon, 4 Nephi, Joseph Smith—History, and the Articles of Faith.

## LONGEST BOOKS

Psalms—150 chapters, 2,461 verses, and 43,743 words.
Alma—63 chapters.
Jeremiah—52 chapters.
Ezekiel—48 chapters.

---

‡ Skousen, Paul, *The Skousen Book of Mormon World Records* (Springville, Utah: Cedar Fort, Inc., 2004), 151–62.

The scriptures are filled with outstanding heroes and role models, but they also have their fair share of horrific villains we love to hate. Here are a few of the nastiest villains in the scriptures. We can roughly place them into four categories: murderers of family, killers of prophets, mass murderers, and deceivers and betrayers.

## MURDERERS OF FAMILY

Laman and Lemuel were bad dudes because they rejected their father's teachings, beat and bound their younger brother Nephi, and murmured all the way to America. But at least they did not murder their own family members. Taking an innocent life is wicked enough, but with the family being central to the Creator's plan of happiness, turning on your own family members is especially egregious. Unfortunately, the scriptures have a number of such villains:

**CAIN**—Our fraternity of fratricide begins with Cain. The phrase "raising Cain" came about because Cain was such a troublemaker. I pity his mother, Eve. Can you imagine keeping up with Cain's mischief as a toddler? As an adult, it was bad enough that Cain took shortcuts with his sacrifices and offerings, but then in jealousy, he killed his brother Abel and lied about it to God's face. "Am I my brother's keeper?" (Genesis 4:9).

As punishment for the world's first murder, Cain was cursed with a mark and became "a fugitive and a vagabond in the earth" (Genesis 4:14). Cain and his wife "loved Satan more than God," and the Lord said to him, "From this time forth thou shalt be the father of his lies; thou shalt be called Perdition" (Moses 5:24, 28). But Cain seemed to wallow in his wickedness and glory in Satan's secrets: "And Cain said: Truly I am Mahan, the master of this great secret, that I may murder and get gain. Wherefore Cain was called Master Mahan, and he gloried in his wickedness" (Moses 5:31).

**JEHORAM**—But why kill just one brother when you can kill six! When good King Jehoshaphat died, the crown of Judah passed to his eldest son, Jehoram. But this wasn't good enough for the 32-year-old new monarch. He looked at his six brothers, who had received from their father "great gifts of silver, and of gold, and of precious things," and realized he needn't settle for just a kingdom when he could have it all! Besides, it was always handy to eliminate rivals for the throne. So the greedy and bloodthirsty Jehoram "strengthened himself, and slew all his brethren with the sword" (2 Chronicles 21:1–5).

**ABIMELECH**—So Cain killed his brother Abel, and Jehoram killed his six brothers, but Abimelech, son of Jerubbaal, did even worse.

WHO ARE THE WORST VILLAINS IN SECULAR HISTORY? RANKER.COM SHARES A SURVEY, WHICH MORE THAN 12,000 PEOPLE HAVE WEIGHED IN ON, THAT IDENTIFIES THE "ALL-TIME WORST PEOPLE IN HISTORY." NUMBER ONE IS NAZI FÜHRER ADOLPH HITLER, WITH SOVIET DICTATOR JOSEPH STALIN AS NUMBER TWO, AND KHMER ROUGE THUG POL POT AS NUMBER THREE. OSAMA BIN LADEN CLOCKS IN AS WORST PERSON NUMBER FOUR, AND UGANDAN GENOCIDAL DICTATOR IDI AMIN ROUNDS OUT THE TOP FIVE.[‡] COMBINED, THESE FIVE HAVE BROUGHT ABOUT THE DEATH OF MORE THAN 21 MILLION PEOPLE AND THE SUFFERING OF MILLIONS MORE IN THE TWENTIETH AND TWENTY-FIRST CENTURIES.[‡‡]

[‡]The All-Time Worst People in History," Ranker.com, accessed January 27, 2014, http://www.ranker.com/crowdranked-list/the-all-time-worst-people-in-history.
[‡‡] Pierro Scaruffi, "The Worst Genocides of the 20th and 21st Centuries," accessed January 23, 2014, http://www.scaruffi.com/politics/dictat.html.

To secure his kingly throne, he hired some mercenaries to help him, and he "went unto his father's house at Ophrah, and slew his brethren the sons of Jerubbaal, being threescore and ten persons, upon one stone." That's the needless death of 70 brothers! Apparently, all were massacred except Jotham, the youngest brother, "for he hid himself" (Judges 9:5).

Well, God was not pleased with this mass fratricide at all: "Then God sent an evil spirit . . . that the cruelty done to the threescore and ten sons of Jerubbaal might come, and their blood be laid upon Abimelech their brother, which slew them" (Judges 9:23–24). This, as you can imagine, did not end well for Abimelech. He was chased to and fro, and in the end, "a certain woman cast a piece of a millstone upon Abimelech's head, and all to brake his skull." This mortally wounded Abimelech, but he did not want to be defeated by a girl, a huge indignity in his mind, so he called to his young armor bearer and said, "Draw thy sword, and slay me, that men say not of me, A woman slew him. And his young man thrust him through, and he died. . . . Thus God rendered the wickedness of Abimelech, which he did unto his father, in slaying his seventy brethren" (Judges 9:53–54, 56).

**HEROD THE GREAT**—The dastardly deeds of Herod I, Roman client king of Judea, are many. Historians have described him as "the evil genius of the Judean nation"[51] and have said he was "prepared to commit any crime in order to gratify his unbounded ambition."[52] The Bible Dictionary notes that "his reign was disgraced by many acts of cruelty. In a fit of jealousy he had his wife, whom he dearly loved, put to death; later on he had her two sons, Alexander and

---

51 H. Graetz, *History of the Jews*, vol. 2 (Philadelphia: The Jewish Publication Society of America, 1893), 77, http://archive.org/stream/historyofje02grae#page/n7/mode/2up.
52 "Herod I, (Surnamed the Great)," *Jewish Encyclopedia*, accessed January 23, 2014, http://jewishencyclopedia.com/articles/7598-herod-i.

Aristobulus, also murdered." Later, he "had Antipater, another of his own sons, put to death."

Though Herod's maniacal murdering of his own family put him in this category, he could actually qualify for any of the other grotesque groupings in this chapter. Herod was the jealous king who was deeply troubled upon hearing that a babe in Bethlehem was the child of prophecy destined to be king of the Jews. He "was exceeding wroth, and sent forth, and slew all the children that were in Bethlehem, and in all the coasts thereof, from two years old and under" (Matthew 2:16). The Massacre of the Innocents, as it came to be known, surely put Herod high on the list of villains in the scriptures.

## KILLERS OF PROPHETS

"Yea, wo unto this people, because of this time which has arrived, that ye do cast out the prophets," Samuel the Lamanite chastised, "and do mock them, and cast stones at them, and do slay them, and do all manner of iniquity unto them, even as they did of old time" (Helaman 13:24). Among the sinister sinners of scriptures are those wicked souls who killed the prophets of God.

**JEZEBEL**—At the top of the list of wicked prophet killers is Jezebel, the Phoenician princess who married King Ahab of the Northern Kingdom of Israel and seduced him and his kingdom into idolatry. She was bad news from the start. When her husband was upset with Naboth for refusing to sell him his vineyard, Jezebel arranged for false witnesses to testify against Naboth, resulting in him being stoned to death. Just to get a vineyard!

Regarding the prophets, "Jezebel slew the prophets of the Lord" and worked to hunt them down, like Emperor Palpatine in *Star Wars* hunting down the Jedi Knights. Obadiah hid some men of God in a cave, but an angry Jezebel specifically threatened Elijah (see 1 Kings 18, 19). Ultimately, Elijah prophesied directly against her: "In the portion of Jezreel shall dogs eat the flesh of Jezebel," he cried. "And the carcase of Jezebel shall be as dung upon the face of the field . . . so that they shall not say, This is Jezebel" (2 Kings 9:36–37).

Jezebel did not like this at all and continued to stir up her husband, King Ahab, to "work wickedness in the sight of the Lord" (1 Kings 21:25). But in the end, Jezebel's servants threw her from the balcony, and she was devoured by the dogs until her carcass was unrecognizable, just as Elijah had foretold: "And they went to bury her: but they found no more of her than the skull, and the feet, and the palms of her hands" (2 Kings 9:35). Wow. Her fingers were even gone, just the palms of her hands remaining. Brutal!

**WHO ARE THE WORST VILLAINS OF HOLLYWOOD?** IN JUNE 2003, THE AMERICAN FILM INSTITUTE RELEASED THEIR RANKINGS OF THE NASTIEST VILLAINS IN MOVIE HISTORY. TOPPING THE LIST WAS THE CANNIBAL DR. HANNIBAL LECTER (*SILENCE OF THE LAMBS*), FOLLOWED BY NORMAN BATES (*PSYCHO*), AND DARTH VADER (*STAR WARS*). THE WICKED WITCH OF THE WEST (*WIZARD OF OZ*) AND NURSE RATCHET (*ONE FLEW OVER THE CUCKOO'S NEST*) ROUNDED OUT THE TOP FIVE. THE REST OF THE TOP FIFTY INCLUDED VILLAINS LIKE NUMBER 10, THE QUEEN (*SNOW WHITE AND THE SEVEN DWARVES*); NUMBER 18, THE SHARK (*JAWS*); NUMBER 39, CRUELLA DE VIL (*101 DALMATIANS*); NUMBER 40, FREDDY KRUEGER (*A NIGHTMARE ON ELM STREET*); AND NUMBER 45 THE JOKER (*BATMAN*).‡ IN THE DECADE SINCE THAT LIST WAS RELEASED, WE HAVE ALSO MET ON THE BIG SCREEN LORD VOLDEMORT (*HARRY POTTER*), BANE (*THE DARK KNIGHT RISES*), AND SAURON (*LORD OF THE RINGS*).‡

‡ See "Good and Evil Rival for the Top Spots in AFI's 100 Years . . . 100 Heroes and Villains," AFI.com, accessed January 23, 2014, http://www.afi.com/100years/handv.aspx.

**HERODIAS**—This villainess is a bad one. Perhaps it was the convoluted gene pool that messed up this Jewish princess because Herodias's father was the son of Herod the Great (remember the one we just talked about?), and her mother was the daughter of Herod's sister Salome I. It's fun to be your own cousin! But it gets worse. For a time, Herodias was married to her uncle,  Herod II (also known as Herod Phillip in Mark 6:17). Then, after divorcing him, she married another uncle, Herod Antipas. So Herodias was not only Herod the Great's granddaughter but also his daughter-in-law *twice*.

With all of this incest in the royal family of Judah, it's easy to see why the prophets would cry foul. John the Baptist came to the court of Herod Antipas and said, "It is not lawful for thee to have thy brother's wife" (Mark 6:18). This sent Herodias fuming. Who was this wilderness-dwelling holy man to tell the royal house of Herod how to run their affairs? How dare he! Herodias wanted John the Baptist dead: "Therefore Herodias had a quarrel against him, and would have killed him" (Mark 6:19). But her new husband realized that killing John the Baptist would be politically unwise, so he just put him in prison as a compromise. Herod Antipas "feared the multitude, because they counted [John the Baptist] as a prophet" (Matthew 14:5).

Awhile later, Herod Antipas was enjoying a birthday feast, and in came Salome, the seductive daughter of his new wife, Herodias, and Herodias's former husband, Herod II. Now, realize, Salome is not only Herod Antipas's new step-daughter, but she is also his niece. Salome danced a seductive dance, known in later histories as the Dance of the Seven Veils, which filled Herod with such lust that he vowed to give her whatever she wanted.

> And she went forth, and said unto her mother, What shall I ask? And she said, The head of John the Baptist.

And she came in straightway with haste unto the king, and asked, saying, I will that thou give me by and by in a charger the head of John the Baptist.

And the king was exceeding sorry; yet for his oath's sake, and for their sakes which sat with him, he would not reject her.

And immediately the king sent an executioner, and commanded [John the Baptist's] head to be brought: and he went and beheaded him in the prison,

And brought his head in a charger, and gave it to the damsel: and the damsel gave it to her mother. (Mark 6:24–28)

It's bad enough that Herodias exploits her daughter to achieve her hateful desire, but when the motive is to kill a prophet, it is especially heinous. A special place in hell surely awaits.

**CAIAPHAS**—The greatest prophet, of course, was the Savior Himself, so His murderers certainly make this list. There are a number of people who share the blame for crucifying our Lord, but the chief instigator is the Jewish high priest Caiaphas. As leader of the Sanhedrin, Caiaphas plotted with his fellow elders to remove the threat to their power called Jesus of Nazareth: "Then assembled together the chief priests, and the scribes, and the elders of the people, unto the palace of the high priest, who was called Caiaphas, And consulted that they might take Jesus by subtilty, and kill him" (Matthew 26:3–4). Caiaphas told the group that Jesus must be killed to preserve their status: "It is expedient for us, that one man should die for the people, and that the whole nation perish not" (John 11:50).

Once Jesus was captured, they took Him to "Caiaphas the high priest, where the scribes and the elders were assembled" (Matthew 26:57). There, Caiaphas conducted a kangaroo court, ridiculous in its lack of legitimate witnesses that Jesus had done anything wrong. They bound our Lord, beat Him, "spit in his face, and buffeted him; and others smote him with the palms of their hands, Saying, Prophesy unto us, thou Christ, Who is he that smote thee?" (Matthew 26:67–68).

Caiaphas was sly enough to know that to put Christ to death, they couldn't merely charge Him with blasphemy. After all, the Romans, who had the authority to perform capital punishment, did not care for the Jews' religious quibbles. Caiaphas had to get Jesus to say something treasonous against Rome. So he had Jesus brought to Pontius Pilate, the Roman governor, and reported that Christ's crime was treason and that He claimed to be king of the Jews and that He refused to recognize Roman authority.

**WHO'S GOING TO HELL?** ACCORDING TO THE BARNA RESEARCH GROUP OF VENTURA, CALIFORNIA, 71 PERCENT OF AMERICAN ADULTS BELIEVE IN HELL. HOWEVER, ONLY ½ OF 1 PERCENT BELIEVE THEY ARE GOING TO HELL AFTER THEY DIE, WITH 64 PERCENT BELIEVING THEY WILL GO TO HEAVEN (THE REST BELIEVE IN REINCARNATION, THAT THE SOUL ENDS AT DEATH, OR ARE UNSURE).[‡]

"And Jesus stood before the governor: and the governor asked him, saying, Art thou the King of the Jews? And Jesus said unto him, Thou sayest" (Matthew 27:11). Caiaphas now had the technicality that could put Jesus to death. His band of Pharisees led the crowd in, clamoring to Pilate, "Crucify him, crucify him" (Luke 23:21). And the Savior was put to death.

Nephi learned in vision of those who would orchestrate the death of Jesus. He called them "the more wicked part of the world" and noted "there is none other nation on earth that would crucify their God" (2 Nephi 10:3).

---

‡ Barna Group, "Americans Describe Their Views about Life After Death," Oct. 21, 2003, https://www.barna.org/barna-update/article/5-barna-update/128-americans-describe-their-views-about-life-after-death#.UkR7Vr7nZMs.

**KING NOAH**—King Noah was the gluttonous son of King Zeniff in the Book of Mormon. Not only did he overtax the people, encourage idolatry and whoredoms, and become a wine-bibber, but King Noah also killed the prophet. He and his priests hated the prophet Abinadi's bold words of rebuke and calls to repentance, so Noah sentenced Abinadi to death.

After the bound Abinadi received his death sentence, he said, "I will suffer even until death, and I will not recall my words, and they shall stand as a testimony against you. And if ye slay me ye will shed innocent blood, and this shall also stand as a testimony against you at the last day" (Mosiah 17:10). Abinadi spoke with such conviction that Noah,

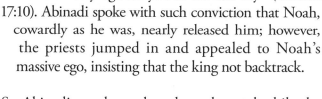

cowardly as he was, nearly released him; however, the priests jumped in and appealed to Noah's massive ego, insisting that the king not backtrack.

So Abinadi was burned at the stake, and while the flames licked his flesh, the dying prophet prophesied to King Noah, "Ye shall suffer, as I suffer, the pains of death by fire" (Mosiah 17:18).

Later, when the Lamanites attacked King Noah's city, Noah fled like a coward into the wilderness with those men who listened to him and left their families to save their own lives: "Now it came to pass that the king commanded them that all the men should leave their wives and their children, and flee before the Lamanites" (Mosiah 19:11).

Eventually, the men who ran away with Noah wanted to go back to check on their families, but "the king commanded them that they should not return." This final act of selfishness and cowardice did not go over well and led to the end of Noah and the fulfillment of Abinadi's prophesy: "And they were angry with the king, and caused that he should suffer, even unto death by fire" (Mosiah 19:20).

**MOB IN CARTHAGE**—There are numerous villains in the Doctrine and Covenants—from apostates and mobs to corrupt judges and Missouri Governor Lilburn W. Boggs, who issued the nefarious Extermination

Order—but in the category of prophet killers, we have to call out the cowardly mob at Carthage. They were, in the words of John Taylor, "an armed mob—painted black—of from 150 to 200 persons," and they martyred not just the Prophet Joseph Smith but also his brother Patriarch Hyrum Smith on June 27, 1844. The deaths of these men were a result of a "conspiracy of traitors and wicked men; and their *innocent blood* on the floor of Carthage jail is a broad seal affixed to 'Mormonism' that cannot be rejected by any court on earth" (D&C 135:1, 7).

Before being killed, Joseph Smith fired off a few rounds in self-defense. The Prophet shot William Gallaher in the face, John Wills in the arm, and William Voras in the shoulder. With their wounds giving them away, these three, plus a Mr. Allen, were all indicted in the murders of Joseph and Hyrum. However, they fled the county and were never brought to trial.[53] As the original lyrics of William W. Phelps's poem "Praise to the Man" read: "Long shall his blood, which was shed by assassins, / Stain Illinois, while the earth lauds his fame."[54]

## MASS MURDERERS

Some of the worst villains in the scriptures were, frankly, mass murderers. They killed large groups of people to accomplish their selfish goals. Shiz, a monster in the book of Ether, was one of those. Gadianton and Nehor are others whose actions and "secret combinations" resulted in massive death and destruction. Below are a few more of this ilk.

**DOEG THE EDOMITE**—Described as "the chiefest of the herdmen that belonged to Saul," Doeg the Edomite was eager to please his master and not afraid to massacre innocent people (1 Samuel 21:7). When he heard that some local priests were helping Saul's rival David, "he fell upon the priests, and slew on that day fourscore and five persons that did wear a linen ephod" (1 Samuel 22:18). But his lust for blood did not end with the 85 priests he killed, and in Nob,

---

53 Dallin H. Oaks and Marvin S. Hill, *Carthage Conspiracy: The Trial of the Accused Assassins of Joseph Smith*, (Urbana: University of Illinois Press, 1975), 52, 53, 79.
54 George D. Pyper, *Stories of the Latter-day Saint Hymns, Their Authors, and Composers*, (Salt Lake City: Deseret Book, 1939), 100.

the city of the priests, he massacred "both men and women, children and sucklings, and oxen, and asses, and sheep, with the edge of the sword" (1 Samuel 22:19).

**LAWYERS AND JUDGES OF AMMONIHAH**—Among other mass murderers in the scriptures are the leaders of the Book of Mormon city of Ammonihah. We learn that "Satan had gotten great hold upon the hearts of the people of the city of Ammonihah" and that their lawyers and judges were the worst of them (Alma 8:9). They rejected Alma and Amulek's teachings and were so angry with them that they "bound them with strong cords, and took them before the chief judge of the land" (Alma 14:4). The chief judge had no mercy on them and incited the people to cast out the men who did believe the prophet's words and follow them and stone them.

As for the families of those believers, their fate was worse: "And they brought their wives and children together, and whosoever believed or had been taught to believe in the word of God they caused that they should be cast into the fire" (Alma 14:8). In their rage, these wicked men not only burned these innocent people alive, but they tossed their scriptures into the fire as well: "And it came to pass that they took Alma and Amulek, and carried them forth to the place of martyrdom, that they might witness the destruction of those who were consumed by fire. And when Amulek saw the pains of the women and children who were consuming in the fire, he also was pained" (Alma 14:9–10).

The chief judge then came and smacked Alma and Amulek on their cheeks and taunted them, saying, "After what ye have seen, will ye preach again unto this people, that they shall be cast into a lake of fire and brimstone?" (Alma 14:14). He threw them back in prison, where he and the other judges visited and harassed them more. Ultimately, God helped Alma and Amulek escape and punished the wicked people of Ammonihah by allowing a Lamanite army to storm the city and fulfill every bad prophecy against that wicked city:

And the people of Ammonihah were destroyed; yea, every living soul of the Ammonihahites was destroyed, and also their great city, which they said God could not destroy, because of its greatness.

But behold, in one day it was left desolate; and the carcasses were mangled by dogs and wild beasts of the wilderness.

Nevertheless, after many days their dead bodies were heaped up upon the face of the earth, and they were covered with a shallow covering. And now so great was the scent thereof that the people did not go in to possess the land of Ammonihah for many years. (Alma 16:9–11)

## TRAITORS

In Dante's *Inferno*, the Ninth Circle of Hell, the lowest place one could go, is Treachery. These are people who aren't just fraudulent but who betray

## WHO'S GOING TO THE CELESTIAL KINGDOM?

CERTAINLY, IT'S A TOUGH PATH FOR ANY SCRIPTURAL VILLAIN TO TURN IT AROUND AND REACH FOR THE HIGHEST HEAVEN, BUT THOSE OF US ON A MORE STABLE PATH COULD STILL MAKE IT THERE. A SURVEY OF 1,300 LDS YOUNG WOMEN SHOWS THAT 55.4 PERCENT BELIEVE THERE WILL BE MORE WOMEN THAN MEN IN THE CELESTIAL KINGDOM.[‡]

BUT LDS DEMOGRAPHERS ARE SHOWING THAT BASED ON THE FACT THAT CHILDREN WHO DIE BEFORE THE AGE OF ACCOUNTABILITY (AGE 8) AUTOMATICALLY GO TO THE CELESTIAL KINGDOM, THERE COULD ALREADY BE MANY MORE MALES THERE. HISTORIC CHILD MORTALITY RATES SHOW THAT MALES ARE BIOLOGICALLY THE WEAKER SEX, AND THERE ARE AN ESTIMATED 1.7 BILLION MORE BOYS WHO HAVE DIED UNDER AGE 8 IN HUMAN HISTORY THAN GIRLS. "WITH SO MANY CELESTIALIZED MALES AVAILABLE IN POSTMORTAL EXISTENCE, IT MAY BE LESS SURPRISING IN THE LONG-TERM PERSPECTIVE THAT WOMEN WHO SURVIVE PAST AGE EIGHT APPEAR TO BE MORE RELIGIOUS THAN THE SURVIVING MEN," THE STUDY POINTS OUT. WITHOUT MORE ADULT WOMEN MAKING IT TO THE CELESTIAL KINGDOM, "A BALANCED SEX RATIO WOULD BE IMPOSSIBLE."[‡‡]

---

‡ "LDS Young Women Survey," July 22, 2013, http://ldsywsurvey.wordpress.com/.
‡‡ "'In the Heavens, Are Parents Single?' Report No. 1" *Dialogue: A Journal of Mormon Thought*, vol. 17, no. 1, (Spring 1984): 84–86; see also SteveP "It's Raining Men: Celestial Demographics (Again)," *By Common Consent*, Dec. 1, 2008, http://bycommonconsent.com/2008/12/01/its-raining-men-celestial-demographics-again/.

a special relationship—their friends, their master, their Father. These traitors in the scriptures are aptly described in Dante's explanation.

## AMALICKIAH—

Within the pages of the Book of Mormon, none is more treacherous than Amalickiah. He is described as "a large and a strong man" who was so "desirous to be a king" that he would say anything, do anything, betray anyone to make it to the top (Alma 46:3–4). First, the "flattering words of Amalickiah" persuaded many to leave the Church and join his monarchist effort, creating an "exceedingly precarious and dangerous" situation for the Nephite nation (Alma 46:7). Second, after Captain Moroni gave Amalickiah's supporters a whippin', Amalickiah and his remaining loyalists ran to the land of Nephi, where they "did stir up the Lamanites to anger against the people of Nephi." Here, he hatched the next step in his plan, because Amalickiah was a "very subtle man to do evil" (Alma 47:1, 4).

He convinced the king of the Lamanites to give him an army to go force-recruit the Lamanite deadbeats who didn't want to fight the Nephites one more time. Led by Lehonti, this group of Lamanites who did not want to fight holed up on Mount Antipas and would not budge. Amalickiah finally lured Lehonti to a secret meeting during the night, where he struck his treacherous deal. Amalickiah would let Lehonti's band surround his army during the night, and he would surrender his army "if [Lehonti] would make [Amalickiah] a second leader over the whole army" (Alma 47:13).

So now that Amalickiah was second in command to an even larger army, the army began marching back to the king of the Lamanites. Along the way, this power-hungry Nephite gradually poisoned Lehonti until he keeled over. As second in command, Amalickiah became head of the army.

His next act of treachery took place outside the Lamanite capital of Nephi. The king of the Lamanites came out onto the field with his servants to welcome Amalickiah on his triumphant return. Amalickiah sent his servants to greet the king with a knife to the heart, and they quickly cried that the king's servants had killed the king. "Amalickiah pretended to be wroth" and sent men to pursue the innocent—but accused and terrified—servants of the king (Alma 47:27). "And thus Amalickiah, by his fraud, gained the hearts of the people" and entered the city of Nephi with ease (Alma 47:30–31).

Amalickiah's next act of treachery was to persuade the queen of the Lamanites that her husband had indeed been killed by his own servants: "And it came to pass that Amalickiah sought the favor of the queen, and took her unto him to wife; and thus by his fraud, and by the assistance of his cunning servants, he obtained the kingdom" (Alma 47:35). With the entire Lamanite kingdom at his command, Amalickiah wreaked havoc on the Nephite nation in years of continual warfare. Though killed in the end, Amalickiah caused unspeakable damage and pain along the way.

**JUDAS ISCARIOT**—Once inside Dante's Ninth Ring of Hell, Treachery, there are four rounds. Round 4, the most dastardly, is called Judecca after the great traitor of the New Testament, Judas Iscariot. As one of the Twelve Apostles called by Christ, Judas was tasked with being treasurer of the group of disciples and "had the bag," as they say. Judas seemed to have a problem with greed and was very upset when Mary (sister of Martha) used expensive ointment on Jesus's feet: "Why was not this ointment sold for three hundred pence,

and given to the poor?" he cried. His fellow Apostle John knew Judas's character and told us the real motive: "This he said, not that he cared for the poor; but because he was a thief, and had the bag, and bare what was put therein" (John 12:5–6).

With such character flaws, Judas Iscariot easily fell when he saw an opportunity to exploit. It was no secret among the disciples that "the chief priests and scribes sought how they might kill" Jesus. And Satan easily planted the sinister idea in Judas's mind to sell his Master for money: "Then entered Satan into Judas surnamed Iscariot."

Judas, in his greed, embraced the Satanic suggestion and "went his way, and communed with the chief priests and captains, how he might betray him unto them. And they were glad, and covenanted to give him money. And he promised, and sought opportunity to betray him unto them in the absence of the multitude" (Luke 22:2–6).

The infamous betrayal took place after the Passover supper and after Jesus had finished the Atonement in the Garden of Gethsemane. One of the most selfish acts in history followed the greatest selfless act in all of history! Judas led the mob to the garden, "went before them, and drew near unto Jesus to kiss him. But Jesus said unto him, Judas, betrayest thou the Son of man with a kiss?" (Luke 22:47–48).

For 30 pieces of silver, Judas Iscariot betrayed his Master and our Lord. Wracked with guilt, Judas ended up committing suicide. His treachery immortalized his villainy.

**LUCIFER**—The greatest villain in the scriptures, of course, is the devil himself. Lucifer's name means "Shining One," "Lightbringer," or "Son of the Morning." He was originally "an angel of God who was in authority in the presence of God," but he rejected Heavenly Father's plan, rebelled against Jehovah, and persuaded one-third of the hosts of heaven to follow him. He "was thrust down from the presence of God and the Son, And was called Perdition, for the heavens wept over him—he was Lucifer, a son of the morning. And we beheld, and lo, he is fallen! is fallen, even a son of the morning!" (D&C 76:25–27). That is the great tragedy of Satan—the distance he fell from being one of the shining stars to being the greatest adversary of God's plan.

"And the great dragon was cast out, that old serpent, called the Devil, and Satan, which deceiveth the whole world: he was cast out into the earth, and his angels were cast out with him" (Revelation 12:9).

The evil he has wrought cannot be adequately catalogued, for his temptations range from persuading Eve to partake of the fruit of good and evil to tempting you with today's unkind thought. But the devil and all of the villains of the scriptures have been overcome: "O the greatness of the mercy of our God, the Holy One of Israel!" the Book of Mormon prophet Jacob said. "For he delivereth his saints from that awful monster the devil, and death, and hell, and that lake of fire and brimstone, which is endless torment" (2 Nephi 9:19).

# Nine

# EPIC JOURNEYS

There are memorable expeditions, voyages, and journeys throughout the scriptures. These are adventures that make Boy Scout 50-milers seem like a Sunbeam's walk to the drinking fountain. We're going to take a closer look at ten epic journeys. Some notable ones, such as Moses leading the children of Israel out of Egypt to the promised land, didn't make the cut. Sure, the Israelites journeyed for forty years in the wilderness, but wandering from Egypt to Palestine really wasn't a long trek. The following epic journeys are listed in order of shortest to longest.

## 10. THE JOURNEY OF THE FIRST CHRISTMAS (700 MILES)

It is the era in history when a decree went out from Caesar Augustus that all the world should be taxed. Joseph the carpenter took Mary, his new bride, and began the trek south from Nazareth to the City of David—Bethlehem. The path they most likely took was a four- or five-day journey of 92 miles: "It would have taken them southeast across the Jezreel Valley, connecting with the Jordan Valley, then level or slightly down in elevation all the way to Jericho, then up through the Judaean Desert to Jerusalem and Bethlehem," BYU professor D. Kelly Ogden, who actually walked the route, described. He pointed out that Jericho was the lowest city on the globe, and "from Jericho's desert to Bethlehem is an uphill hike of 3,500 feet. How exhausted Mary must have been! How anxious Joseph must have been to find a comfortable room at the inn!"[55]

55 D. Kelly Ogden, "The Road to Bethlehem," *Ensign*, Dec. 1995, 23.

But the special Christmas family's journey was not through. After being warned in a dream of King Herod's forces coming to slaughter all the babies, Joseph "took the young child and his mother by night, and departed into Egypt" (Matthew 2:14). It was a logical place to go—outside of Herod's domain but still part of the Roman Empire, and the road provided relatively safe travel. The Holy Family probably joined a caravan for the 300-mile journey, a common way to travel safely for longer distances back then. After a season in Egypt, Joseph was again instructed in a dream to relocate his family, this time taking them home to Nazareth in Galilee. When Joseph and Mary brought the young Jesus into the old homestead and carpenter shop of Nazareth, it had been several years and over 700 miles since their Christmas odyssey began.

## 9. NEHEMIAH RETURNS HOME FROM PERSIA (1,000 MILES)

When Judah was invaded, Jerusalem sacked, and the Jews captured and taken to Babylon in 597 B.C., the Jews were forced 554 miles east (as the crow flies). In 538 B.C., the Persians conquered Babylonia, and the decree of Cyrus allowed the Jews to begin returning to Palestine. Some Jews initially stayed in the East, including Nehemiah, who rose to an important position in King Artaxerxes of Persia's court. The king of Persia ruled from the city of Susa, in modern Iran, hundreds of miles east of Babylon.

In 444 B.C., Nehemiah asked for and received permission from Artaxerxes to return to Jerusalem to rebuild the city walls. The king appointed Nehemiah governor of the province of Judah, and Nehemiah headed west across the desert to Jerusalem to

assist Ezra in the rebuild. As the crow flies, it is 770 miles from Susa to Jerusalem, but the meandering of the desert caravan paths would have made that journey closer to 1,000 miles. At a typical caravan's pace of 20 miles per day, it would have taken Nehemiah about 50 days to traverse the Zagros Mountains, cross the Tigris and Euphrates Rivers, and endure the Syrian Desert. Remarkably, after 12 years as governor, Nehemiah returned to Susa for a season and then made the 1,000-mile trek back to Jerusalem a second time!

## 8. PIONEER TREK TO UTAH (1,300 MILES)

One of the most epic journeys in the scriptures is recorded in the Doctrine and Covenants—the pioneer trek to the Great Basin. "Let every man use all his influence and property to remove this people to the place where the Lord shall locate a stake of Zion," Brigham Young instructed the Saints (D&C 136:10). From Nauvoo, Illinois, to the valley of the Great Salt Lake, the journey clocks in at over 1,300 miles—across the Mississippi River, through the dusty Great Plains, along the Platte River, over the Continental Divide, and into the Rocky Mountains.

Unlike many of the epic journeys in the scriptures, this one was

**GLOBE-CIRCLING MISSION TOUR, 1920–21** DAVID O. MCKAY, THEN AN APOSTLE, COMPLETED A WORLDWIDE TOUR OF THE MISSIONS OF THE CHURCH BY ASSIGNMENT FROM THE FIRST PRESIDENCY. WITH HIS COMPANION, HUGH J. CANNON, HE TRAVELED AN AMAZING 61,646 MILES AS HE CIRCUMNAVIGATED THE PLANET. IN HAWAII, ELDER MCKAY HAD A VISION THAT LED TO THE FOUNDING OF BYU–HAWAII YEARS LATER. THEY DEDICATED CHINA FOR THE PREACHING OF THE GOSPEL AND VISITED SAMOA, TONGA, NEW ZEALAND, AND PALESTINE. THE GLOBE-TROTTING APOSTLE LEFT UTAH ON DECEMBER 4, 1920 AND ARRIVED BACK IN UTAH ON CHRISTMAS EVE 1921.‡

‡ Hugh J. Cannon, *To the Peripheries of Mormondom: The Apostolic Around-the-World Journey of David O. McKay, 1920–1921*, ed. Reid L. Neilson (Salt Lake City: University of Utah Press, 2011).

not only long and arduous, but it also involved thousands of people. In addition to the vanguard company of 1847, more than 70,000 Mormon pioneers traveled the trail before the coming of the transcontinental railroad in 1869. This journey was especially epic for the legendary handcart pioneers, who made up less than 10 percent of the pioneers but who endured especially difficult trials of weather and stamina: "Of all the stories of American pioneers and settlers," President John F. Kennedy said, "none is more inspiring than the Mormon trail."[56]

## 7. ZION'S CAMP (2,000 MILES)

When the Saints in Jackson County, Missouri, were suffering from mob persecution and being driven from their homes, the Lord commanded Joseph Smith to get hundreds of men and "gather yourselves together unto the land of Zion" (D&C 103:22). The group of about 200 men and some women and children, known as Zion's Camp, left Kirtland, Ohio, on May 4, 1834. They marched through the states of Indiana and Illinois and crossed the Mississippi River into Missouri on June 4. By the end of June, they reached the beleaguered Saints then seeking refuge in Clay County.

### SAINTS ABOARD THE *BROOKLYN*

THE LONGEST PASSAGE A MORMON EMIGRANT COMPANY MADE WAS ABOARD THE SHIP *BROOKLYN*. CHURCH LEADERS DIRECTED SAMUEL BRANNAN TO CHARTER A SHIP TO CARRY SAINTS FROM THE EASTERN UNITED STATES TO THE WEST COAST AND RECRUITED 70 MEN, 68 WOMEN, AND 100 CHILDREN FOR THE TRIP. THEY SAILED OUT OF NEW YORK HARBOR ON FEBRUARY 4, 1846—THE SAME DAY THE MORMON EXODUS FROM NAUVOO BEGAN. THE SIX-MONTH VOYAGE TOOK THE PASSENGERS OF THE *BROOKLYN* SOUTH THROUGH THE ATLANTIC OCEAN, ACROSS THE EQUATOR, AROUND CAPE HORN AT THE BOTTOM OF SOUTH AMERICA, WITH A BRIEF STOP AT THE JUAN FERNÁNDEZ ISLANDS, NORTH THROUGH THE PACIFIC EQUATOR, WITH ANOTHER STOP IN HAWAII, AND THEN FINALLY TO YERBA BUENA (SAN FRANCISCO), WHERE THEY DOCKED ON JULY 29, 1846. THIS AMAZING VOYAGE OF NEARLY 24,000 MILES CLAIMED 10 OF THE SHIP'S 238 PASSENGERS.

---

56 John F. Kennedy, "Address in Salt Lake City at the Mormon Tabernacle," Sep. 26, 1963.

Negotiations failed to return the Saints to Jackson County, and the Prophet received a revelation to not fight because Zion would have to be redeemed at a later date when the Saints were better prepared. A cholera epidemic broke out among the camp, and the group was formally disbanded on July 25, 1834. Most of the survivors (14 died) traveled the 1,000 miles back to Kirtland.

Remarkably, the nearly 2,000-mile roundtrip the men of Zion's Camp endured was significantly longer than the pioneer trek from Nauvoo to Salt Lake, yet many questioned if it accomplished anything. "Was Zion's Camp a catastrophe? Perhaps, but it was not the unmitigated disaster that it appears to be," Joseph Smith scholar Richard Bushman said. "Most camp members felt more loyal to Joseph than ever, bonded by their hardships. The future leadership of the Church came from this group."[57] Epic journeys have a way of strengthening people and determining who has the faith to endure.

## 6. PAUL'S JOURNEY TO ROME (2,300 MILES)

"But by the grace of God I am what I am," the Apostle Paul said (1 Corinthians 15:10). And what is he? Oh, simply the greatest missionary of all time and second only to the Savior in shaping Christianity's place in the world, according to much of Christendom.

"He is about 5 foot high; very dark hair; dark complexion, dark skin; large Roman nose," the Prophet Joseph Smith said of the Apostle Paul.

He had a "sharp face; small black eyes, penetrating as eternity; round shoulders; a whining voice, except when elevated and then it almost resembles the roaring of a lion. He was a good orator."[58]

---

57 Richard Lyman Bushman and Lyndon W. Cook, eds., *Joseph Smith: Rough Stone Rolling* (New York: Knopf, 2005), 247.

58 Andrew F. Ehat and Lyndon W. Cook, *The Words of Joseph Smith* (Provo, Utah: Religious Studies Center, Brigham Young University, 1980), 59.

Paul went on numerous missionary journeys that would each qualify for this list. His first missionary journey took him north to Syria, modern Turkey, and the island of Cyprus. His second mission took him beyond those lands to Greece and Macedonia. His third missionary journey revisited many of these lands. But it was his 2,300-mile journey to Rome that became his longest trek. He sailed north from Caesarea to Myra in Turkey, westward to the Fair Havens on the isle of Crete, on to Malta, where he was shipwrecked, then north between Sicily and the toe of the Italian boot, and finally to Rome.

**OTHER APOSTOLIC MISSIONS** PAUL WASN'T THE ONLY APOSTLE TO TRAVEL FAR IN THE SERVICE OF OUR LORD. IT IS BELIEVED THAT PETER ALSO WENT TO ROME, THAT JAMES PREACHED IN SPAIN, AND THAT JOHN MINISTERED IN MODERN TURKEY AND WROTE THE BOOK OF REVELATION ON THE ISLE OF PATMOS. THERE ARE TRADITIONS THAT SPEAK OF ANDREW PREACHING IN CYPRUS, MALTA, ROMANIA, GEORGIA, AND THE UKRAINE. PHILIP TAUGHT IN GREECE, SYRIA, AND TURKEY. BARTHOLOMEW IS SAID TO HAVE GONE ON A MISSION TO INDIA AND BEEN MARTYRED WHILE PREACHING IN ARMENIA. THOMAS ALSO SPREAD THE GOSPEL TO INDIA. MATTHEW SUPPOSEDLY TAUGHT IN SYRIA, MACEDONIA, AND PERSIA. JAMES, THE SON OF ALPHAEUS, WAS APPARENTLY MARTYRED ON A MISSION TO EGYPT. THADDEUS TAUGHT IN SYRIA AND AS FAR WEST AS LIBYA. TRADITIONS HAVE SIMON THE ZEALOT PREACHING IN PERSIA, ARMENIA, EGYPT, AND EVEN BRITAIN. MATTHIAS TAUGHT AS FAR NORTH AS MODERN GEORGIA ON THE EASTERN SHORES OF THE BLACK SEA.

After two years of imprisonment in Rome, Paul was released (see Acts 28:30). He then spent the next four years traveling through the Mediterranean world—perhaps as far west as Spain—preaching before again being taken prisoner to Rome, where he was martyred in the spring of AD 65.[59]

## 5. MORMON BATTALION (3,200 MILES)

As the pioneers crossed the plains from Nauvoo and headed toward the Rockies, over 500 men were enlisted to fight for the U.S. Army in the war with Mexico. The Mormon Battalion, as it came to be known, underwent the longest infantry march in U.S. military

---

59 See Bible Dictionary, s.v., "Paul."

history. The battalion was accompanied by 30 women, 23 of whom served as laundresses, and 51 children.

The U.S. enlisted the Mormon Battalion on July 16, 1846, and assigned it to the Army of the West under the direction of tough General Kearney. They marched the 167 miles south from Council Bluffs, Iowa, to Fort Leavenworth to gear up for the grueling trek west to the Pacific. They left Fort Leavenworth on August 30, 1846, and marched 1,900 miles to San Diego, California—crossing the modern states of Kansas, Oklahoma, Colorado, New Mexico, and Arizona, and dipping briefly into Mexico. They endured dust storms and drought, carved wagon trails later instrumental in the settlement of the American Southwest, survived the "Battle of the Bulls," and captured Tucson, Arizona, without firing a shot.

Even after they reached San Diego on January 29, 1847, they were not through, as most wound their way north to Sacramento and over the Sierra Nevadas eastward to meet with the main group of the Saints just arriving in the valley of the Great Salt Lake—an additional 1,200 miles. Most of the Mormon Battalion ended up walking more than 3,200 miles from Council Bluffs, Iowa, to San Diego and then up to Salt Lake City—an epic journey indeed!

## 4. MULEKITES ACROSS THE OCEAN (7,000 MILES)

The Book of Mormon tells of the Nephites coming upon other refugees from Israel in about 250 B.C.: "Mosiah discovered that the people of Zarahemla came out from Jerusalem at the time that Zedekiah, king of Judah, was carried away captive into Babylon [about 587 B.C.]. And they journeyed in the wilderness, and were brought by the hand of the Lord across the great waters, into the land where Mosiah discovered them" (Omni 1:15–16).

These people of Zarahemla are called Mulekites because of their leader Mulek, son of Zedekiah, and there are a couple of clues that they crossed the Atlantic rather than the Pacific Ocean. First, the Mulekites encountered the only Jaredite survivor of the battle at the hill Ramah, which was described as being near the eastern sea. Also, the city of Mulek was on the eastern seacoast (see Alma 51:26).

It appears as though they took their journey west from Jerusalem, through the Judean wilderness to the Mediterranean coast, then aboard a ship also heading westward through the Great Sea, beyond the Strait of Gibraltar and into the Atlantic Ocean, and on to the Americas, a distance of more than 7,000 miles.

**HAGOTH'S SHIPS TO THE SOUTH SEAS**
WE READ IN THE BOOK OF MORMON OF HAGOTH, "AN EXCEEDINGLY CURIOUS MAN" WHO BUILT SHIPS AND SENT THEM FILLED WITH COLONISTS INTO THE WEST SEA (ALMA 63:5–8). THEIR JOURNEYS INTO THE PACIFIC OCEAN WERE TRULY EPIC VOYAGES. GEORGE Q. CANNON, HEBER J. GRANT, AND OTHER CHURCH LEADERS HAVE LONG TAUGHT THAT THE BLOOD OF THE PACIFIC ISLANDERS IS RICH WITH THE ANCESTRY OF HAGOTH'S SEAFARING PEOPLE. THIS GROUP, OR THEIR DESCENDANTS, EVENTUALLY MADE IT AS FAR AS NEW ZEALAND—6,000 MILES ACROSS THE PACIFIC! IN A STATEMENT TO THE MAORIS OF NEW ZEALAND, PRESIDENT JOSEPH F. SMITH SAID, "I WOULD LIKE TO SAY TO YOU BRETHREN AND SISTERS . . . YOU ARE SOME OF HAGOTH'S PEOPLE, AND THERE IS NO PERHAPS ABOUT IT!"‡

## 3. APOSTOLIC MISSION TO BRITAIN (8,000 MILES)

The Quorum of the Twelve Apostles had two very successful missions to Britain—the first from 1837–38 and the second from 1839–41. The second makes our list of epic journeys, as the brethren traveled from Nauvoo, Illinois, to Preston, England, and back again—a land and sea journey that totaled more than 8,000 miles! "Let them depart to go over the great waters, and there promulgate my gospel, the fulness thereof, and bear record of my name" (D&C 118:4).

---

‡ William A. Cole and Elwin W. Jensen, *Israel in the Pacific* (Salt Lake City: Genealogical Society, 1961), 388.

Making this journey across half a continent and the Atlantic Ocean especially epic were the humble circumstances of the Apostles and their families when they left on their journey in the summer of 1839. Brigham Young and Heber C. Kimball were both so sick and weak when they departed that they needed help getting into their wagon. They also left behind very ill wives and children.

Heber describes their departure:

> It seemed to me as though my very inmost parts would melt within me at leaving my family in such a condition, as it were almost in the arms of death. I felt as though I could not endure it. I asked the teamster to stop, and said to Brother Brigham, "This is pretty tough, isn't it; let's rise up and give them a cheer." We arose, and swinging our hats three times over our heads, shouted: "Hurrah, hurrah for Israel." Vilate [his wife], hearing the noise, arose from her bed and came to the door. She had a smile

**ORSON HYDE'S MISSION TO JERUSALEM**
THOUGH NOT MENTIONED IN THE SCRIPTURES, AN EPIC JOURNEY TOOK PLACE DURING DOCTRINE AND COVENANT TIMES WHEN JOSEPH SMITH SENT ELDER ORSON HYDE OF THE TWELVE TO PALESTINE. CALLED TO GO IN THE CONFERENCE OF APRIL 1840, ELDER HYDE TRAVELED FROM NAUVOO TO EUROPE, ARRIVING IN LIVERPOOL, ENGLAND. AFTER SOME TIME IN ENGLAND, HE CONTINUED ON TO AMSTERDAM, NETHERLANDS; BRUSSELS, BELGIUM; STRASBOURG, FRANCE; THEN DOWN THE DANUBE RIVER BY BOAT TO CONSTANTINOPLE. THEN HE SAILED TO SMYRNA, TURKEY; BEIRUT, LEBANON; ALEXANDRIA, EGYPT; AND FINALLY TO THE HOLY LAND. ON THE MORNING OF OCTOBER 24, 1841, HE PASSED THROUGH THE GATES OF JERUSALEM AND CLIMBED THE MOUNT OF OLIVES, WHERE, AS AN APOSTLE OF THE LORD, HE DEDICATED PALESTINE FOR THE GATHERING OF THE JEWS. AFTERWARD, HE PREACHED IN EGYPT AND GERMANY FOR A FEW MONTHS AND THEN JOINED A GROUP OF BRITISH CONVERTS FOR THE TRIP HOME ACROSS THE ATLANTIC. ORSON HYDE ARRIVED HOME IN DECEMBER 1842 AFTER AN EPIC MISSION OF 32 MONTHS AND NEARLY 20,000 MILES.

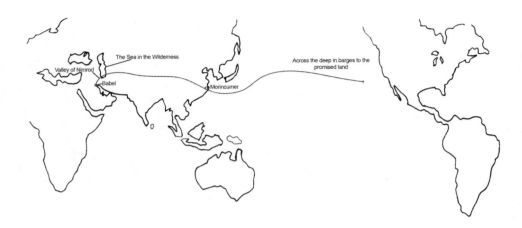

on her face. Vilate and Mary Anne Young cried out to us: "Goodbye, God bless you."[60]

## 2. JAREDITES TRAVEL TO AMERICA (14,000 MILES)

Although the Jaredite journey probably wasn't as long as the Lehite journey from the Middle East to America, it is easy to argue that it was more arduous. The Jaredites in the Book of Mormon left the Tower of Babel and "went down into the valley which was northward" (Ether 2:1) and then farther inland on the Asian continent, "into that quarter where there never had man been" (Ether 2:5). "They did travel in the wilderness, and did build barges, in which they did cross many waters" (Ether 2:6). Many LDS scholars suppose the "many waters" to be the Caspian Sea—earth's largest lake and, indeed, "many waters" in the ancient phraseology.[61]

The Jaredites did not "stop beyond the sea in the wilderness" (Ether 2:7) but rather continued, presumably eastward, along what would later be known as the Silk Road until "the Lord did bring Jared and his brethren forth even to that great sea which divideth the lands" (Ether 2:12). They called the place Moriancumer and pitched their tents there for four years, somewhere on Asia's east coast. The brother of Jared communed

---

60 Orson F. Whitney, *Life of Heber C. Kimball*, 3d ed. (Salt Lake City: Bookcraft, 1967), 265–66.

61 See Hugh W. Nibley, *Lehi in the Desert/The World of the Jaredites/There Were Jaredites* (Salt Lake City: Bookcraft, 1952); see also research by the Olive Leaf Foundation, http://www.achoiceland.com/unknown_quarter.

**WERE THE WISE MEN FROM AMERICA?** AT CHRISTMASTIME, WE REMEMBER THAT "THERE CAME WISE MEN FROM THE EAST TO JERUSALEM" (MATTHEW 2:1). MANY SUPPOSE THESE STAR-FOLLOWING HOLY MEN WERE SIMPLY MAGI FROM PERSIA, BUT JEFFREY D. HOLT PROVIDES A TANTALIZING ALTERNATIVE. HE PROPOSES THE IDEA THAT THE THREE WISE MEN MAY HAVE BEEN SAMUEL THE LAMANITE AND THE SONS OF HELAMAN—NEPHI AND LEHI. AFTER ALL, IT IS STRANGE THAT THESE THREE MOST PROMINENT RELIGIOUS LEADERS OF THEIR DAY SUDDENLY DISAPPEARED FROM THE LAND NOT LONG BEFORE THE MESSIAH WAS BORN (SEE 3 NEPHI 1:3 AND HELAMAN 16:8). CLEARLY, THESE PROPHETS KNEW OF THE STAR AND SIGNS OF CHRIST'S BIRTH. IN FACT, SAMUEL GAVE US THE ONLY SCRIPTURAL PROPHESY OF THE STAR THAT THE WISE MEN LATER FOLLOWED (SEE HELAMAN 14:5). LEGEND ALSO HAS IT THAT ONE OF THE WISE MEN HAD DARKER SKIN—SAMUEL THE LAMANITE? THE BOOK OF MORMON PROPHETS ALSO DIDN'T KNOW OF THE BIRTH BEING IN BETHLEHEM BUT KNEW IT WOULD BE IN THE JERUSALEM AREA, WHICH EXPLAINS WHY THEY FIRST WENT THERE (SEE ALMA 7:10; MATTHEW 2:1). WE READ IN THE BOOK OF MORMON OF ANGELS APPEARING TO "WISE MEN" WITH "GLAD TIDINGS OF GREAT JOY" BEFORE THE SAVIOR'S BIRTH (HELAMAN 16:14). WERE THESE WISE MEN REPRESENTATIVES OF THE "OTHER SHEEP" IN THE AMERICAS, AND HAD THEY TRAVELED AROUND THE GLOBE TO BE SPECIAL WITNESSES OF OUR LORD'S BIRTH? IF THEY WERE, THEIR 15,000-MILE JOURNEY FROM THE EAST TO HONOR THE CHRIST CHILD IN BETHLEHEM WOULD TRULY HAVE BEEN EPIC!‡

with the Lord on a high mountain by the coast, and some LDS scholars suppose that the mountain could be Laoshan, a 3,716-foot-tall peak that is the highest coastal mountain in China and has been held sacred for thousands of years.[62] It certainly fits the description of a mountain of "exceeding height" on that coast (Ether 3:1).

And this incredible 6,000-mile journey over the entire continent of Asia was just the beginning! The Jaredites then climbed into eight barges and drifted and were driven about by the wind and were tossed

---

62 See "Jared, His Brother, and Their Friends: Enduring a 344-Day Ocean Voyage," aChoiceLand.com, accessed January 23, 2014, http://www.achoiceland.com/344_day_voyage.

‡ See Jeffrey D. Holt's unpublished manuscript of *Return to Jerusalem: Book of Mormon Wise Men* in author's possession.

about the sea for 344 days until they reached the promised land of America (see Ether 6). They would have traveled about 8,000 miles as they crossed the ocean, moving along at an average of 23 miles per day, which is very similar to the average drift speeds of the oceanic currents between China and the Americas.

After this epic voyage halfway around the world, by land and by sea, it is no wonder that "when they had set their feet upon the shores of the promised land they bowed themselves down upon the face of the land, and did humble themselves before the Lord, and did shed tears of joy before the Lord, because of the multitude of his tender mercies over them" (Ether 6:12).

## 1. LEHITES TO AMERICA (15,000 MILES)

The longest known journey in the scriptures is the epic adventure of Lehi and Sariah and their family, who left Jerusalem in 600 B.C. They traveled 180 miles south into the wilderness "near the shore of the Red Sea" (1 Nephi 2:5). After returning a couples of times to Jerusalem for the brass plates and Ishmael's family, the party went "in a south-southeast direction" to a place they called Shazer (1 Nephi 16:13). They

continued along the "most fertile parts of the wilderness, which were in the borders near the Red Sea" (1 Nephi 16:14). At one point, "Ishmael died, and was buried in the place which was called Nahom" (1 Nephi 16:34). When they resumed the journey in the wilderness, the Lehites "did travel nearly eastward

from that time forth," and they "did sojourn for the space of many years, yea, even eight years in the wilderness" until they came to a delightful land by the seashore that they called Bountiful (1 Nephi 17:1, 4–5).

It was a brutal eight-year journey, with men, women, children, and newborns: "And we did travel and wade through much affliction in the wilderness," Nephi reported. "And our women did bear children in the wilderness" (1 Nephi 17:1). Most LDS scholars figure the land of Bountiful was in the modern country of Oman in the bottom of the Arabian Peninsula, a 600-mile journey from the Red Sea.[63] After a season in the land Bountiful on the seashore, they "did all go down into the ship" that Nephi had built and "did put forth into the sea and were driven forth before the wind towards the promised land" (1 Nephi 18:6, 8).

**GLOBETROTTING PRESIDENT HINCKLEY** PRESIDENT GORDON B. HINCKLEY TRAVELED MORE THAN ONE MILLION MILES AND MINISTERED IN 160 COUNTRIES IN HIS TIME AS A GENERAL AUTHORITY, MORE THAN ANYONE IN CHURCH HISTORY. "NO MAN IN THE HISTORY OF THE CHURCH HAS TRAVELED SO FAR TO SO MANY PLACES IN THE WORLD WITH SUCH A SINGLE PURPOSE IN MIND," PRESIDENT BOYD K. PACKER SAID OF PRESIDENT HINCKLEY. "TO PREACH THE GOSPEL, TO BLESS AND LIFT UP THE SAINTS, AND TO FOSTER THE REDEMPTION OF THE DEAD."‡

"When they left the Arabian Peninsula, the land of Bountiful, if they followed the course that later Arab sailors followed, they would have gone virtually straight east across the Indian Ocean," BYU emeritus professor of anthropology John L. Sorenson says. "And that required that it was during the season of the monsoon, when winds are from the south but veering over toward the Indian Peninsula."

63 Even the writers of Church manuals seem to support that the Lehite land journey was confined to the Arabian Peninsula. (See *Book of Mormon Student Manual* 1 Nephi 15–17, Salt Lake City: The Church of Jesus Christ of Latter-day Saints, 1996, http://www.ldsces.org/manuals/book-of-mormon-institute-student-manual/bm1996-02-1ne-2-4.asp).

‡ "President Gordon B. Hinckley: Stalwart and Brave He Stands," *Ensign*, June 1995, 13.

"Nephi, no doubt, kept close to shore when he could," Professor Kelly DeVries adds. "This was not something that was just tradition among shippers, this was for safety and for resupply purposes."

These two scholars believe Lehi's party then traveled through a strait around Sri Lanka, then over to Thailand and the Malaysian Peninsula, and then eastward into the vast Pacific. "The place where the westerly winds caused by El Niño would go would be mostly south of the equator," Sorenson says. "When Nephi gets to the islands of the South Pacific, he can make small jumps between these islands," DeVries adds. "And then he has to make the jump to the New World, and that would have been the most frightening part. That's when the bravery and seamanship comes in. There's no island for refuge."[64]

From Oman to the western shore of the Americas is an epic sailing voyage that, combined with their land journey, resulted in a trip of around 15,000 miles.

64 In S. Kent Brown and Peter Johnson, "Journey of Faith: Ships," Maxwell Institute, accessed January 23, 14, http://alex.farmsresearch.com/publications/books/?bookid=127&chapid=1508.

# Ten

# MONEY AND FORTUNE

Guys have always been intrigued with money—the stuff it can buy and the game of accumulating it. We're also curious as to who has it and who doesn't.

The scriptures have a lot to say about wealth. Money righteously earned is a gift from God. "Every man also to whom God hath given riches and wealth," we read in Ecclesiastes 5:19, "and hath given him power to eat thereof, and to take his portion, and to rejoice in his labour; this is the gift of God."

We are also told that money itself is not bad, but the love of money is: "For the love of money is the root of all evil" (1 Timothy 6:10). Moroni warns us about the last days: "For behold, ye do love money, and your substance, and your fine apparel, and the adorning of your churches, more than ye love the poor and the needy, the sick and the afflicted" (Mormon 8:37).

Jesus taught that it is difficult—but not impossible—for the wealthy to get to heaven. "It is easier for a camel to go through the eye of a needle," He said, "than for a rich man to enter into the kingdom of God" (Mark 10:25). When the disciples were astonished by this, Jesus clarified by saying, "With men this is impossible; but with God all things are possible" (Matthew 19:26).

Jacob gives us great advice on how to maintain this balance: "And after ye have obtained a hope in Christ ye shall obtain riches, if ye seek them; and ye will seek them for the intent to do good—to clothe the naked, and to feed the hungry, and to liberate the captive, and administer relief to the sick and the afflicted" (Jacob 2:19).

So with all that as context, let's look at some of the wealthiest individuals in the scriptures.

## OLD TESTAMENT FORTUNES

**ABRAHAM**—Strangely, Abraham received much of his wealth as gifts from Egypt's Pharaoh, who was striving to win the hand of Abraham's wife (who Pharaoh thought was Abraham's sister): "And he entreated Abram well for her sake: and he had sheep, and oxen, and he asses, and menservants, and maidservants, and she asses, and camels" (Genesis 12:16). When Abraham and Sarah left Egypt, they were doing pretty well! "And Abram was very rich in cattle, in silver, and in gold" (Genesis 13:2). He went on to leverage this nest egg into a substantial domain in the promised land.

**ISAAC**—As Abraham's heir, Isaac had a great starting point. But due to his righteousness, his flocks and fields really boomed: "Then Isaac sowed in that land, and received in the same year an hundredfold: and the Lord blessed him. And the man waxed great, and went forward, and grew until he became very great: For he had possession of flocks, and possession of herds, and great store of servants: and the Philistines envied him" (Genesis 26:12–14). Isaac became so wealthy that the jealous Philistines filled his wells with dirt and begged him to move away.

**NAHAB**—Known as a man of Maon, with property in Carmel, was the wealthy but stingy Nahab: "The man was very great, and he had three thousand sheep, and a thousand goats" (1 Samuel 25:2). He refused to help David when his armies were passing through and instead stayed home and got drunk while feasting like a king. But his wife, Abigail, snuck out and entreated David and his band, and her gifts give us a glimpse of Nahab's wealth: "Two hundred loaves, and two bottles of wine, and five sheep ready dressed, and five measures of parched corn, and an hundred clusters of raisins, and two hundred cakes of figs" (1 Samuel 25:18). Ten days after the incident, the Lord struck Nahab dead for his stinginess and Abigail was invited to become one of David's wives.

**SOLOMON**—As a new king, Solomon asked the Lord not for riches and power but for wisdom. The Lord was pleased with this and gave him wisdom, but He also rewarded Solomon's righteousness: "And I have also given thee that which thou hast not asked, both riches, and honour: so that there shall not be any among the kings like unto thee all thy days" (1 Kings 3:13). And the Lord was not kidding. Solomon became the wealthiest man in the history of the world to that point.

**WHO ARE THE WEALTHIEST FICTIONAL CHARACTERS? BELIEVE IT OR NOT, FORBES RECENTLY RAN A LIST OF THE WEALTHIEST FICTIONAL CHARACTERS, WITH SCROOGE MCDUCK ($65.4 BILLION) AND SMAUG THE DRAGON FROM THE HOBBIT ($54.1 BILLION) TOPPING THE LIST. OTHER MULTIBILLIONAIRES IN FANTASYLAND INCLUDE IRON MAN TONY STARK ($12.4 BILLION), BATMAN BRUCE WAYNE ($9.2 BILLION), RICHIE RICH ($5.8 BILLION), THE SIMPSONS' MR. BURNS ($1.5 BILLION), MR. MONOPOLY FROM THE BOARD GAME ($1.2 BILLION), THE GREAT GATSBY'S JAY GATSBY ($1 BILLION), AND MORE.‡**

Because of Solomon's tremendous wisdom, the rich and famous from all over the ancient world trekked to Jerusalem to call upon him. And when they did, they showered him with more riches and gifts: "So king Solomon exceeded all the kings of the earth for riches and for wisdom" (1 Kings 10:23).

The gifts were extraordinary: "And they brought every man his present, vessels of silver, and vessels of

‡ David M. Ewalt, "The 2013 Forbes Fictional Fifteen," *Forbes*, Jul. 31, 2013.

gold, and garments, and armour, and spices, horses, and mules, a rate year by year" (1 Kings 10:25).

The queen of Sheba was one of those visitors who showered gifts on him: "And she gave the king an hundred and twenty talents of gold, and of spices very great store, and precious stones: there came no more such abundance of spices as these which the queen of Sheba gave to king Solomon" (1 Kings 10:10).

But Solomon's wealth wasn't just in gifts; he was also a brilliant merchant in trade. He controlled spice trades and had his navies bring back gold, silver, precious stones, ivory, apes, peacocks, and more. His palace was bedecked in gold, from the ivory throne covered with the finest gold down to the dining ware. Solomon was so rich that he didn't even use silver in his palace because he had so much gold.

Solomon's wealth was so unbelievable that it made typically valued items commodities: "And the king made silver to be in Jerusalem as stones, and cedars made he to be as the sycomore trees that are in the vale, for abundance" (1 Kings 10:27). King Solomon typically ranks high in lists of wealthiest historical figures and is without question the wealthiest in the scriptures.

**JEHOSHAPHAT**—The fourth king of Judah, Jehoshaphat, "sought to the Lord God of his father, and walked in his commandments." Consequently, "the Lord stablished the kingdom in his hand; and all Judah brought to Jehoshaphat presents; and he had riches and honour in abundance." Even neighboring peoples showered the righteous king with gifts: "Also some of the Philistines brought Jehoshaphat

# How King Solomon's wealth stacks up (all amounts in today's dollars)

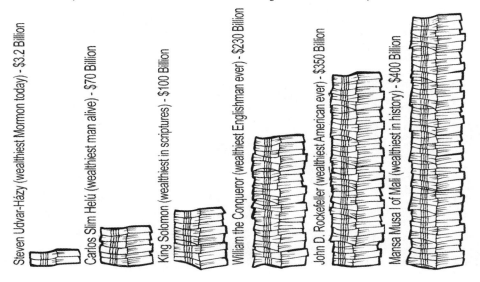

Steven Udvar-Házy (wealthiest Mormon today) - $3.2 Billion

Carlos Slim Helú (wealthiest man alive) - $70 Billion

King Solomon (wealthiest in scriptures) - $100 Billion

William the Conqueror (wealthiest Englishman ever) - $230 Billion

John D. Rockefeller (wealthiest American ever) - $350 Billion

Mansa Musa I of Mali (wealthiest in history) - $400 Billion

presents, and tribute silver; and the Arabians brought him flocks, seven thousand and seven hundred rams, and seven thousand and seven hundred he goats." So what did Jehoshaphat do with this amazing wealth? Being a conservative fellow, he built up fortifications to protect the kingdom of Judah and replenished the kingdom's food storage: "And Jehoshaphat waxed great exceedingly; and he built in Judah castles, and cities of store" (2 Chronicles 17:4–5, 11–12).

**HEZEKIAH**—The thirteenth king of Judah, Hezekiah was also greatly blessed materially for humbling himself before God and removing idols from the temple in Jerusalem. "And Hezekiah had exceeding much riches and honour: and he made himself treasuries for silver, and for gold, and for precious stones, and for spices, and for shields, and for all manner of pleasant jewels." He was so rich he had to construct treasuries just to house it all. He even built "storehouses also for the increase of corn, and wine, and oil; and stalls for all manner of beasts, and cotes for flocks." Seriously, when you have so much corn you have to build storehouses to keep it all in, that's rich. Hezekiah was so wealthy he even had the means to build the Broad Wall to help protect Jerusalem and the famous Hezekiah's Tunnel that is still there nearly 3,000 years later. "Moreover he provided him cities, and possessions of flocks and herds in abundance: for God had given him substance very much" (2 Chronicles 32:27–29).

**AHASUERUS**—The Persian king in the book of Esther, also known in history as Xerxes the Great, was a rich man. As the fourth king of kings in the Persian Empire, he ruled a domain that stretched from India to Greece down to Ethiopia, the largest empire the world had seen to that point. Xerxes had the treasure to fund enormous building projects, including the Gate of all Nations and the Hall of a Hundred Columns in the city of Persepolis. He finished the palace his father, Darius I, began, as well as an enormous treasury, and while he was at it, he built himself a new palace twice the size of his father's. The book of Esther gives one telling glimpse of his opulence when Xerxes throws a *six-month-long* feast for all of the nobles and princes of the 127 provinces he ruled over, where he "shewed the riches of his glorious kingdom" (Esther 1:1–4).

**JOB**—The book of Job begins by describing the great wealth of the title character: "His substance also was seven thousand sheep, and three thousand camels, and five hundred yoke of oxen, and five hundred she asses, and a very great household; so that this man was the greatest of all the men of the east" (Job 1:3). Of course, he loses it all, along with his family and health, as Satan is allowed to test Job's loyalty to God. But when he passes the test, God pours out even more riches upon Job in return, exactly doubling his wealth from before: "So the Lord blessed the latter end of Job more than his beginning:

for he had fourteen thousand sheep, and six thousand camels, and a thousand yoke of oxen, and a thousand she asses" (Job 42:12). If Job was regarded as the "greatest of all the men of the east" earlier, one can imagine his regard when his net worth doubled!

## RICH MEN IN THE NEW TESTAMENT

**ZACCHAEUS**—The head tax collector in Jericho, Zacchaeus "was the chief among the publicans, and he was rich." Of course he was. Tax collectors in ancient Israel tended to take more than their fair share of commissions on what they gathered and were universally despised for it. After Zacchaeus dined with Jesus and was converted, he pledged to give half of his means to the poor and to return any taxes he collected "from any man by false accusation" fourfold (Luke 19:1–9).

### THE RICH YOUNG RULER—

This young man was the one who asked our Lord, "Good Master, what good thing shall I do, that I may have eternal life?" When Jesus listed the key commandments, this young man of wealth and means replied, "All these things have I kept from my youth up: what lack I yet?" (Matthew 19:16, 21). The Master, seeing the young man's costly attire and perhaps sensing his love for his wealth, said, "One thing thou lackest: go thy way, sell whatsoever thou hast, and give to the poor, and thou shalt have treasure in heaven: and come, take up the cross, and follow me." But this was too much for this young ruler and his riches, "and he was sad at that saying, and went away grieved: for he had great possessions" (Mark 10:21–22). This was a rich dude who simply could not part with his great wealth.

**JOSEPH OF ARIMATHÆA**—After the crucifixion of our Lord, "there came a rich man of Arimathæa, named Joseph, who also himself was

Jesus' disciple" (Matthew 27:57). He successfully begged Pilate for the Savior's body and had it properly buried in his own private sepulchre. Not only does the Bible state outright that Joseph was rich, but his having a prepaid deluxe burial chamber also shows that Joseph of Arimathæa was one of the wealthier men in the New Testament. If it weren't for this rich man's generosity, Jesus likely would have been buried in the common graves reserved for criminals who were crucified (see Matthew 27:57–60).

**NICODEMUS**—Friend of Joseph of Arimathæa and fellow Pharisee and member of the ruling Sanhedrin, Nicodemus was one of the very few elites who held sympathies for Jesus of Nazareth. He helped his friend Joseph entomb our Lord: "And there came also Nicodemus, which at the first came to Jesus by night, and brought a mixture of myrrh and aloes, about an hundred pound weight" (John 19:39). Elder James E. Talmage explains, "The odorous mixture was highly esteemed for anointing and embalming, but its cost restricted its use to the wealthy."[65] A hundred pounds' worth was really fit for a king. This man used his wealth to honor the King of Kings.

**ROMAN CENTURION**—The unnamed Roman centurion mentioned in Matthew 8 and Luke 7 had great wealth. Centurions commanded at least 80 Roman soldiers and received significant salaries, typically 17 times that of a legionary soldier.[66] In his generosity, the Roman centurion single-handedly financed a synagogue for the people he brought law and order to. And this guy's faith was as large as his pocketbook—he knew that if Jesus but spoke the word, his servant would be healed: "When Jesus heard these things, he marvelled at him, and turned him about, and said unto the people that followed him, I say unto you, I have not found so great faith, no, not in Israel" (Luke 7:9).

**JOSES BARNABAS**—Mentioned in the book of Acts as a member of the priestly Levite tribe, Joses was from the island nation of

65 James E. Talmage, *Jesus the Christ* (Salt Lake City: Deseret Book, 1983), 617.
66 Earl S. Johnson Jr., *The New Interpreter's Dictionary of the Bible,* vol. 1 (Nashville: Abingdon Press, 2006), 580.

Cyprus and had vast real estate holdings. A believing man, he was totally committed and determined to use his wealth to help the new Church. The Saints at this time were filled with the Holy Ghost and consecrated what they had to helping each other: "And the multitude of them that believed were of one heart and of one soul: neither said any of them that ought of the things which he possessed was his own; but they had all things common." Joses called Barnabas caught the spirit of those apostolic days and "having land, sold it, and brought the money, and laid it at the apostles' feet" (Acts 4:32, 37).

**SIMON THE SORCERER**—This convert had so much money rolling around he tried to buy the priesthood: "Give me also this power, that on whomsoever I lay hands, he may receive the Holy Ghost," he said to Peter. "But Peter said unto him, Thy money perish with thee, because thou hast thought that the gift of God may be purchased with money" (Acts 8:19–20).

## THE WEALTHY IN THE BOOK OF MORMON

**LEHI**—We know that this Book of Mormon patriarch had great treasures because of what he left behind when he took his family into the wilderness. "And he left his house, and the land of his inheritance, and his gold, and his silver, and his precious things" (1 Nephi 2:4). This wealth is further elaborated when his sons go home to get the loot to bargain with Laban for the brass plates: "For behold he [Lehi] left gold and silver, and all manner of riches" (1 Nephi 3:16). All this discussion about Lehi's "land of his inheritance" has led many scholars to presume that Lehi had great property, livestock, and other hereditary wealth. His value was so great that even a mighty man like Laban, with his palace and servants and mini army protecting it all, was jealous of it: "And it came to pass that when Laban saw our property, and that it was exceedingly great, he did lust after it, insomuch that he thrust us out, and sent his servants to slay us, that he might obtain our property" (1 Nephi 3:25). Yes, Lehi had his fortune, but he walked away from it all to dwell in a tent. "And all this he hath done because of the commandments of the Lord" (1 Nephi 3:16).

**JAROM**—As the son of Enos, grandson of Jacob, and great-grandson of Lehi, Jarom hailed from a prominent Nephite family. He was a key member of their society when they began to prosper in the promised land: "And we . . . became exceedingly rich in gold, and in silver, and in precious things," Jarom wrote, "and in fine workmanship of wood, in buildings, and in machinery, and also in iron and copper, and brass and steel, making all manner of tools of every kind to till the ground, and weapons of war." He wrote that he lived in a time when his family and his people saw that the words of the prophets were verified, who said, "Inasmuch as ye will keep my commandments ye shall prosper in the land" (Jarom 1:8–9). And prosper they did!

**KING NOAH**—King Noah was a wicked king who not only gathered his wealth unjustly but spent it frivolously: "And it came to pass that he placed his heart upon his riches, and he spent his time in riotous living with his wives and his concubines." King Noah built his fortune on the backs of the people he was supposed to serve by taxing one-fifth of everything they had "to support himself, and his wives and his concubines; and also his priests, and their wives and their concubines." Noah went on a construction binge, building "many elegant and spacious buildings; and he ornamented them with fine work of wood, and of all manner of precious things, of gold, and of silver, and of iron, and of brass, and of ziff, and of copper; And he also built him a spacious palace, and a throne in the midst thereof, all of which was of fine wood and was ornamented with gold and silver and with precious things." He built towers for lookouts and vast vineyards to support his wine habits. This wicked guy lived the high life—for a time. "And thus they were supported in their laziness, and in their idolatry, and in their whoredoms, by the taxes which king Noah had put upon his people" (Mosiah 11:6–14).

**ZEEZROM**—Not as rich as a king, of course, super-lawyer Zeezrom still amassed quite a fortune. The legal profession at the time of Alma and Amulek was corrupt and set on racking up the billable hours, regardless of how illegitimate: "Now, it was for the sole purpose to get gain, because they received their wages according to their employ, therefore, they did stir up the people to riotings, and all manner of disturbances and wickedness, that they might have more employ, that they might get money according to the suits which were brought before them." And among this crowd, none was more effective than Zeezrom, "a man who was expert in the devices of the devil." Zeezrom could even throw big sums around, like when he offered Amulek 6 onties of silver if he would deny the existence of God. An onti was worth 7 senums, which was equivalent to a measure of barley or a single day's wage for a judge. So the 6 onties Zeezrom threw out there were worth 42 days of a judge's wage (or the equivalent of tens of thousands of dollars in today's world). But Amulek put the rich lawyer in his place: "O thou child of hell, why tempt ye me? . . . Thou knowest that there is a God, but thou lovest that lucre more than him" (Alma 11:20–21, 23–24 ).

**JAREDITE KINGS**—There were a number of Jaredite kings who had great wealth and led their people to prosperity. One was the son of Jared, Orihah, who did "walk humbly before the Lord, and did remember how great things the Lord had done for his father." For this, he and his kingdom were blessed, "and the people began to prosper; and they became exceedingly rich" (Ether 6:28, 30).

**MORMON BUSINESS TITANS** LATTER-DAY SAINTS HAVE DONE EXCEPTIONALLY WELL IN BUSINESS, AND A NUMBER OF CEOs OF MAJOR CORPORATIONS HAVE BEEN MORMONS. A FEW INCLUDE NOLAN ARCHIBALD (BLACK AND DECKER), JERRY ATKIN (SKY WEST AIRLINES) GARY BAUGHMAN (FISHER PRICE), FRANCIS CASH (LA QUINTA), DAVE CHECKETTS (MADISON SQUARE GARDEN), JONATHAN COON (1-800-CONTACTS), STEPHEN R. COVEY (FRANKLIN COVEY), JON HUNTSMAN (HUNTSMAN CHEMICAL), KEVIN KNIGHT (KNIGHT TRANSPORTATION), FRED LAMPROPOULOS (MERIT MEDICAL), STEVE LUND (NUSKIN), J. WILLARD MARRIOTT (MARRIOTT), DAVID NEELEMAN (JET BLUE), SHAWN NELSON (LOVESAC), RAY NOORDA (NOVELL), JAMES QUIGLEY (DELOITTE AND TOUCHE), GEORGE ROMNEY (AMERICAN MOTORS), MITT ROMNEY (BAIN CAPITAL), KEVIN ROLLINS (DELL COMPUTER), ROGER SANT (AES CORP), JAMES L. SORENSON (SORENSON MEDIA), DONALD STAHELI (CONTINENTAL GRAIN), KAY WHITMORE (EASTMAN KODAK), AND MARK WILLIS (TIMES MIRROR).[‡]

---

‡ See the full list at www.famousmormons.net.

Another prosperous king was Emer: "And the house of Emer did prosper exceedingly under the reign of Emer; and in the space of sixty and two years they had become exceedingly strong, insomuch that they became exceedingly rich." We even get a detail of their prosperity: "Having all manner of fruit, and of grain, and of silks, and of fine linen, and of gold, and of silver, and of precious things; And also all manner of cattle, of oxen, and cows, and of sheep, and of swine, and of goats, and also many other kinds of animals which were useful for the food of man. And they also had horses, and asses, and there were elephants and cureloms and cumoms; all of which were useful unto man, and more especially the elephants and cureloms and cumoms" (Ether 9:16–19). King Solomon's apes and peacocks are nothing compared to King Emer's cureloms and cumoms. This guy had wealth *and* cool animals.

Another Jaredite king who led his people to prosperity and riches was Morianton: "And it came to pass that Morianton built up many cities, and the people became exceedingly rich under his reign, both in buildings, and in gold and silver, and in raising grain, and in flocks, and herds, and such things which had been restored unto them" (Ether 10:12).

But not all Jaredite kings were wealthy. Despite his high-tech-sounding name, Com's bubble burst, and his stock as a Jaredite king never rose very high: "And it came to pass that Com drew away the half of the kingdom" (Ether 10:32).

## RICHEST IN THE DOCTRINE AND COVENANTS
**MARTIN HARRIS**—In the early days of the Church, it was said that "Harris was the only man of property or credit known in all Mormondom."[67] Martin inherited and acquired a combined 320 acres in the Palmyra, New York, area and prospered as a farmer and as a merchant of livestock and produce along the Erie Canal. A neighbor described him as "an industrious, hard-working farmer, shrewd in his business calculations, frugal in his habits, and . . . a prosperous man

---

67 Pomeroy Tucker, *Origin, Rise, and Progress of Mormonism* (New York: D. Appleton and Company, 1867), 49.

in the world."[68] One of the Three Witnesses to the Book of Mormon, Martin Harris mortgaged his farm to come up with the $3,000 needed to pay the Grandin Press for the first printing of the Book of Mormon. This was the equivalent of $75,000 in today's dollars. He also gave Joseph Smith $50 to travel to Harmony, Pennsylvania, and he once bought Joseph a fine suit because he thought the Prophet's attire was "inappropriate for a man called of God."[69]

**EDWARD HUNTER**—The second-wealthiest man in West Nantmeal Township, Chester County, Pennsylvania, was Edward Hunter, a

prosperous farmer who inherited vast real estate holdings and lived on a 440-acre farm. When the local interdenominational meetinghouse burned down, he used his property to promptly get it replaced. Befriended by Mormon missionaries, he allowed Joseph Smith to stay with him while he was in the eastern states, and when he was finally baptized in 1840, he was "the wealthiest Mormon convert of that era."[70] Hunter sent thousands of dollars in dry goods to the needy Saints in Nauvoo, and when he left Pennsylvania in 1842 to join

them, he brought $7,000 more. "I took pleasure in assisting him," Hunter said of the Prophet Joseph. "One year he said I had assisted him 15,000 Dollars."[71] Edward Hunter later served as Presiding Bishop from 1851 to 1883.

---

68 Matthew S. McBride, "The Contributions of Martin Harris," The Church of Jesus Christ of Latter-day Saints, January 3, 2013, http://history.lds.org/article/doctrine-and-covenants-martin-harris?lang=eng.

69 Susan Easton Black and Larry C. Porter, "For the Sum of Three Thousand Dollars," *Journal of Book of Mormon Studies*, vol. 14, no. 2 (Provo, Utah: Maxwell Institute, 2005): 4–11, 66–67.

70 Stephen J. Fleming and David W. Grua, eds., "The Impact of Edward Hunter's Conversion to Mormonism in Chester County, Pennsylvania: Henry M. Vallette's 1869 Letter," *Mormon Historical Studies*, 135, http://mormonhistoricsites.org/wp-content/uploads/2013/04/MHS_SPRING-2005_09-EDWARD-HUNTER-CONVERSION.pdf.

71 Michael K. Winder, *Presiding Bishops* (Salt Lake City: Eborn Books, 2003), 57.

**TRIAL BY RICHES** "THE WORST FEAR THAT I HAVE ABOUT [MEMBERS OF THIS CHURCH] IS THAT THEY WILL GET RICH IN THIS COUNTRY, FORGET GOD AND HIS PEOPLE, WAX FAT, AND KICK THEMSELVES OUT OF THE CHURCH AND GO TO HELL. THIS PEOPLE WILL STAND MOBBING, ROBBING, POVERTY, AND ALL MANNER OF PERSECUTION, AND BE TRUE. BUT MY GREATER FEAR FOR THEM IS THAT THEY CANNOT STAND WEALTH; AND YET THEY HAVE TO BE TRIED WITH RICHES, FOR THEY WILL BECOME THE RICHEST PEOPLE ON THIS EARTH."‡ PRESIDENT BRIGHAM YOUNG

**BRIGHAM YOUNG**—Mentioned eight times in the Doctrine and Covenants, the Lion of the Lord would come from humble beginnings to become one of the most prosperous men in the western United States. As a director of numerous business enterprises in the bustling Utah Territory, President Brigham Young acquired an impressive net worth. His homes included the Beehive House and Lion House, the ornate Gardo House, a winter home in St. George, and a farm six miles outside of the city. Of course, this was all to help house his 55 wives and 56 children. When Brigham died in 1877, his estate was worth $1,626,000.[72] Adjusted to today's dollars using the Consumer Price Index, that amount would equal nearly $40 million. And as a real share of the national economy at the time, it would be the equivalent of more than $3 billion today. However, in settling Brigham's estate after his death, they used approximately $1 million to repay loans from the Church, leaving his inheritance somewhat smaller but nonetheless impressive for its day.

72 Glen M. Leonard and James B. Allen, *The Story of the Latter-day Saints* (Salt Lake City: Deseret Book, 1976), 385.
‡ Preston Nibley, *Brigham Young: The Man and His Work* (Salt Lake City: Deseret Book, 1936), 128.

## Eleven

# SPACE AND CELESTIAL SCIENCE

It is no secret that Latter-day guys love space, science, and high tech. There's a Google site for "LDS Astronomers," an LDS *Star Wars* Facebook page, numerous LDS science-fiction writers (most notably Orson Scott Card of *Ender's Game* fame), and Utah has more computers per household than any state in the Union.[73] We've even had Latter-day astronauts, such as Don Lind and Jake Garn, administer the sacrament on the space shuttle. So let's see what the scriptures teach us about space.

## THE BIG PICTURE

Lorenzo Snow taught, "As man now is, God once was; as God now is, so man may be."[74] This profound statement implies that since our God was once a mortal man, He too surely dwelt on an earth with billions of other spirit siblings. If speculation proves correct, many of these have achieved godhood themselves—and that generation was not the first, nor the hundredth, nor the millionth to achieve "immortality and eternal life" (Moses 1:39). How many throughout the eternities have become as Abraham, Isaac, and Jacob, who have "entered into

73 Stephen Ohlemacher, "Utah No. 1 in Homes with Computers," *Deseret News*, Oct. 31, 2005, http://www.deseretnews.com/article/635157158/Utah-No-1-in-homes-with-computers.html?pg=all.

74 Eliza R. Snow, *Biography of Lorenzo Snow* (Salt Lake City: Deseret Book, 1884), 46.

their exaltation, according to the promises, and sit upon thrones, and are not angels but are gods"? (D&C 132:37). It becomes clear that there are an infinite number of heavenly parents stretching forever throughout space and time, eon after eon, infinity upon infinity, unto *gnolaum*, the Hebrew word for eternal (see Abraham 3:18). Even Paul acknowledged that "there be gods many, and lords many . . . but to us there is but one God, the Father" (1 Corinthians 8:5–6).

But the scriptures don't yet reveal all of the secrets of the cosmos. As a young Primary boy of ten, I once opened the Salt Lake phone book and flipped through until I found a General Authority name I recognized: Howard W. Hunter. President Hunter was acting President of the Twelve Apostles at the time, but to me, he was a potential answer to my question. Hiding in my parents' bedroom, I picked up the phone and dialed the number. A woman answered, and after asking my name, she handed the phone to President Hunter.

I told him I had a gospel question, and he said to go ahead and ask. "Elder Hunter," I began, "we know that our Heavenly Father had a Heavenly Father and that He must have had a Heavenly Father and that He must have had one. But where did it all begin? Who was the first one?"

After a brief silence on the other end of the line, President Hunter kindly told me, "Well, Michael, that's something that has not been revealed to us in the scriptures, but someday in the next life, we will know all these things."

I replied with a disappointed "Oh."
He then asked me, "Are you being a good boy?"

**GOD'S COSMIC FUNERALS AND YOU** "SO IT IS, AMID THE VASTNESS OF HIS CREATIONS, GOD'S PERSONAL SHAPING INFLUENCE IS FELT IN THE DETAILS OF OUR LIVES—NOT ONLY IN THE DETAILS OF THE GALAXIES AND MOLECULES BUT, MUCH MORE IMPORTANTLY, IN THE DETAILS OF OUR OWN LIVES. SOMEHOW GOD IS PROVIDING THESE INDIVIDUAL TUTORIALS FOR US WHILE AT THE SAME TIME HE IS OVERSEEING COSMIC FUNERALS AND BIRTHS, FOR AS ONE EARTH PASSES AWAY SO ANOTHER IS BORN. IT IS MARVELOUS THAT HE WOULD ATTEND TO US SO PERSONALLY IN THE MIDST OF THOSE COSMIC DUTIES."‡

---

‡ Neal A. Maxwell, "Becoming a Disciple," *Ensign*, June 1996, 12.

"Yes."

"Do you obey your parents?"

"Yes."

"Are you preparing to go on a mission someday?"

"Yes."

"Those are the most important things," he said. He thanked me for the call, and that was that.

Eight years later, I opened a letter from President Howard W. Hunter calling me to serve as a missionary in Taiwan.

The point is, the scriptures don't tell us everything about the universe, but they do tell us what we need for salvation. However, I don't want to minimize what they say about space; so what do they teach us? It turns out, quite a bit.

## THE KOLOB SYSTEM

The capital of our universe lies at its center, the source of creation and intergalactic government—it is God Himself upon His throne. God's throne sits upon a perfected sphere called simply "the celestial, or the residence of God." The facsimile from the book of Abraham explains, "The celestial [is] the place where God resides" ("A Facsimile from the Book of Abraham, No. 2, Fig. 1"). John the Revelator described the surface of this world as "a sea of glass like unto a crystal . . . [with] a rainbow round about the throne, in sight like unto an emerald" (Revelation 4:3, 6).

"The angels do not reside on a planet like this earth," Joseph Smith said in the Doctrine and Covenants. "But they reside in the presence of God, on a globe like a sea of glass and fire, where all things for their glory are manifest, past, present, and future, and are continually before the Lord. The place where God resides is a great Urim and Thummim" (D&C 130:6–8).

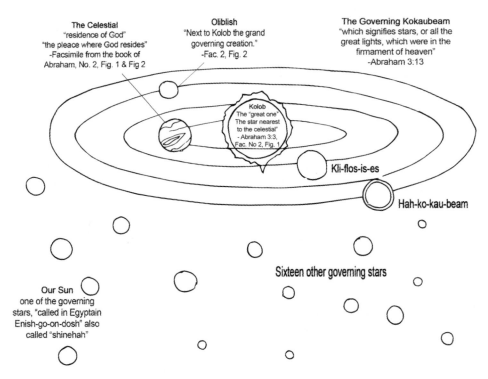

John revealed that the celestial sphere where God lives is also filled with wonderful, intelligent animals that are there to give God praise: "And every creature which is in heaven, and on the earth, and under the earth, and such as are in the sea, and all that are in them." The animals can talk there, and John heard the creatures of our God and King lifting up their voices and saying, "Blessing, and honour, and glory, and power, be unto him that sitteth upon the throne, and unto the Lamb for ever and ever" (Revelation 5:13). John also saw strange beasts around the throne of God praising Him, including some six-winged creatures with multiple eyes. Some of them resembled a lion, another a calf, another a man, and another an eagle (see Revelation 4:6–9). The scriptures note that these were "four individual beasts . . . in the enjoyment of their eternal felicity" (D&C 77:3).

"I suppose John saw beings there of a thousand forms, that had been saved from ten thousand times ten thousand earths like this,—strange beasts of which we have no conception: all might be seen in heaven," Joseph Smith explained. "The grand secret was to show John what

there was in heaven. John learned that God glorified Himself by saving all that His hands had made, whether beasts, fowls, fishes or men; and He will glorify Himself with them."[75]

Latter-day Saints often believe God lives on Kolob, but He doesn't. The scriptures teach us that God and the angels dwell on the celestial planet in the Kolob star system. Kolob is the "great one" of all the stars (Abraham 3:3). It was the "first creation" and is "nearest to the celestial" (Facsimile No. 2, Fig. 1), even "nigh unto the throne of God" (Abraham 3:9). Kolob is "first in government" (Facsimile No. 2, Fig. 1), and Elohim has "set this one to govern all those which belong to the same order as" our planet, earth (Abraham 3:3). Kolob is also "the last pertaining to the measurement of time" (Facsimile No. 2, Fig. 1), which principle Jehovah explained to Abraham in this way:

The moon of our earth "is above or greater than" the earth "in point of reckoning" (Abraham 3:5), for "it rotates on its axis more slowly" (Abraham 3:5, footnote *a*); however, "there shall be another planet whose reckoning of time shall be longer still; And thus there shall be the reckoning of the time of one planet above another, until thou come nigh unto Kolob" (Abraham 3:8–9). This makes sense considering earth rotates on its axis in 24 hours, the moon in 29.5 days, Mercury in 58 earth days, Venus in 243 earth days, etc.

75 Joseph Smith, *Teachings of the Prophet Joseph Smith*, ed. Joseph Fielding Smith (Salt Lake City: Deseret Book, 1974), 291; see also D&C 77:2–4.

Kolob is the universe's standard of time. Her "times and seasons [are] after the manner of the Lord, [for] one revolution [of Kolob is] a day unto the Lord . . . being one thousand years" of earth's years. "This is the reckoning of the Lord's time, according to the reckoning of Kolob" (Abraham 3:4). Technically, however, "all is as one day with God, and time only is measured unto men" (Alma 40:8).

The Lord taught Abraham that "Kokaubeam . . . signifies stars, or all the great lights, which were in the firmament of heaven" (Abraham 3:13). "Kolob is the greatest of all the Kokaubeam," the Lord God explained, "because it is nearest unto me" (Abraham 3:16).

## THE GOVERNING STARS

"Next to Kolob [stands] the next grand governing creation . . . called by the Egyptians Oliblish." It is not clear as to whether Oliblish is a binary star system with Kolob; however, we do know that Oliblish is the next one "near to the celestial, or the place where God resides" (Facsimile No. 2, Fig. 2).

Surpassed only by Kolob in the intergalactic hierarchy, Oliblish has the privilege of "holding the key of power . . . pertaining to other planets" (ibid.); while Kolob has the seemingly superior jurisdiction "to govern all those planets which belong to the same order as" the earth (Abraham 3:9). The "measuring of time" of Oliblish is "one thousand . . . which is equal with Kolob in its revolution and in its measuring of time" (Facsimile No. 2, Fig. 5).

Two other governing stars appear to be Kli-flos-is-es and Hah-ko-kau-beam. They each receive light "from the revolutions of Kolob" (ibid.). It is not entirely clear by the scriptures what their role is, but they seem to help amplify and distribute the light and power emanating from Kolob. It has been revealed that "this planet receives its power through the medium" of these two stars (ibid).

Sixteen other governing stars seem to be part of the upper echelon of ruling heavenly bodies. These borrow their light from Kolob "through the medium of Kae-e-vanrash, which is the grand Key, or, in other words, the governing power."

One of these "is called in Egyptian Enish-go-on-dosh," which "is said by the Egyptians to be the Sun" (ibid.). Elsewhere, the Lord also reveals another name for the sun: "This is Shinehah" (Abraham 3:13). The sun obeys the will of God, as evidenced by the day "the sun stood still in the midst of heaven, and hasted not to go down about a whole day" so Joshua and his armies had time to defeat their enemies. "And there was no day like that before it or after it" (Joshua 10:13–14). On another occasion, God commanded the sun to go backward ten degrees in the sky: "So the sun returned ten degrees, by which degrees it was gone down" (Isaiah 38:8).

Hence, we see 20 primary Kokaubeam (stars) among the stellar hierarchy that light and power our universe. They are Kolob; Oliblish, Kli-flos-is-es; Hah-ko-kau-beam; our sun, Enish-go-on-dosh; and 15 others whose names are not yet revealed to man. Perhaps it was these ruling stars that Lucifer referred to when he made the hollow threat, "I will exalt my throne above the stars of God" (Isaiah 14:13).

## THE CREATOR OF THE UNIVERSE

While the supremacy in the universe is rightly attributed to the Divine Architect, our Heavenly Father, no analysis of the universe would be complete without also examining the colossal contributions of the Almighty Creator, the Only Begotten Son of the Father, Jesus Christ. Old Testament prophets noted that Jehovah created all of the cosmos, not just this earth: "Seek him that maketh the seven stars and Orion," Amos admonished (Amos 5:8). The Great Jehovah is He "which maketh Arcturus, Orion, and Pleiades," Job acknowledged (Job 9:9).

Christ is the power by which all things were made (see D&C 88:6–8), and His light controls and governs these creations. It powers "the light of the sun . . . the light of the moon . . . as also the light of the stars . . . which light proceedeth forth from the presence of God to fill the immensity of

space" (D&C 88:7–12). Perhaps the power of Kae-e-vanrash mentioned earlier is the priesthood, and the Light of Christ, for this "Light . . . is the law by which all things are governed, even the power of God" (D&C 88:14).

Elohim declared to Moses, "And worlds without number have I created; and I also created them for mine own purpose; and by the Son I created them, which is mine Only Begotten" (Moses 1:33). He later emphasized the sheer number of His creations: "The heavens, they are many, and they cannot be numbered unto man; but they are numbered unto me, for they are mine . . . and I know them" (Moses 1:37, 35).

"For behold," the Father said, "there are many worlds that have passed away by the word of my power" (Moses 1:35). Earlier, God told Moses that the "word of my power" meant "the Only Begotten Son" (Moses 1:32). Thus we see that these many worlds have already filled "the measure of [their] creation" through Jesus Christ and have passed on to their next stage of existence (D&C 88:25).

"And as one earth shall pass away, and the heavens thereof even so shall another come," declared the Divine Overseer. "And there is no end to my works," which works are to "bring to pass the immortality and eternal life of man" (Moses 1:38–39).

Of these worlds, God notes that "there are many that now stand, and innumerable are they unto man" (Moses 1:35). Therefore, we see that there are many worlds still in their creation stage, many currently enjoying their mortality, many basking in millennial and paradisiacal glory, and even more still that have already passed away and become celestial kingdoms. Telestial, terrestrial, and celestial worlds abound throughout this vast universe, "and the inhabitants thereof are begotten sons and daughters of God." All through Christ Jesus, "the worlds are and were created" to the glory of the Father (D&C 76:24).

And yet, even though the inhabitants of these other worlds are sons and daughters of God and may be in more advanced states, they do not minister to this world. Joseph Smith taught, "There are no angels who minister to this earth but those who do belong or have belonged to it" (D&C 130:5).

## THE UNIQUENESS OF FLAGSHIP EARTH

"In the beginning God created the heaven and the earth" (Genesis 1:1). From this famous first line of the Bible, we see the genesis of our home planet. Like He did with trillions of worlds before it and trillions more after it, "the Lord . . . created the earth that it should be inhabited; and he . . . created his children that they should possess it" (1 Nephi 17:36).

However, this earth is different from all of the rest. For it is on this blue sphere that the Almighty Creator condescended to be "born of a woman" (Alma 19:13), to "take upon [Him] flesh and blood" (Ether 3:9), and in the humblest of circumstances bring to pass the universal redemption of all of God's children.

This planet also seems to have some of the most wicked and some of the most righteous sons and daughters in the universe dwelling on it. For example, "He who came unto his own was not comprehended," we read. "The light shineth in darkness, and the darkness comprehendeth it not" (D&C 88:48–49).

The crucifiers of the Creator of galaxies are of this world, but so are many righteous people, such as those in Enoch's city of Zion. This city and its people were so righteous that "Zion, in process of time, was taken up into heaven" (Moses 7:21). Enoch enumerated the Lord's creations: "And were it possible that man could number the particles of this earth, yea, millions of earths like this, it would not be a beginning to the number of [His] creations; and [His] curtains are stretched out still." And then in awe, Enoch declared to the Lord, "And thou hast taken Zion to thine own bosom, from all thy creations, from all eternity to all eternity" (Moses 7:30–31). Apparently, among the universe, Zion was no ordinary city. And within the universe, this earth is no ordinary planet either.

Planet earth is a living, growing, spiritual being: "For I, the Lord God, created all things, of which I have spoken, spiritually, before they were naturally upon the face of the earth" (Moses 3:5). The earth itself was, therefore, created spiritually before it was physically organized. The scriptures even tell us of the earth's feelings and emotions and its special affinity with its Creator:

And it came to pass that Enoch looked upon the earth; and he heard a voice from the bowels thereof, saying; Wo, wo is me, the mother of men; I am pained, I am weary, because of the wickedness of my children. When shall I rest, and be cleansed from the filthiness which is gone forth out of me? When will my Creator sanctify me, that I may rest, and righteousness for a season abide upon my face?

And when Enoch heard the earth mourn, he wept, and cried unto the Lord, saying: O Lord wilt thou not have compassion upon the earth? (Moses 7:48–49)

This is the earth that would mourn when her Creator was crucified, "and because of the groanings of the earth, many of the kings of the isles of the sea [were] wrought upon by the Spirit of God, to exclaim: The God of nature suffers" (1 Nephi 19:12).

Like all living entities, the earth, according to God's plan, will eventually die: "The elements shall melt with fervent heat" (Mormon 9:2) and the "earth shall be consumed and pass away" (D&C 29:23), just as countless other worlds have "passed away by the word of [God's] power" (Moses 1:35). But "notwithstanding it shall die, it shall be quickened again . . . and the righteous shall inherit it" (D&C 88:26). Then, the scriptures say, there will be "new heavens and a new earth" (Isaiah 65:17).

"This earth, in its sanctified and immortal state, will be made like unto crystal and will be a Urim and Thummim to the inhabitants who dwell thereon," Joseph Smith told us in the Doctrine and Covenants. "And this earth will be Christ's" (D&C 130:9). "[Then] the earth abideth the law of a celestial kingdom, for it filleth the measure of its creation" (D&C 88:25).

## GODSPEED

For years, scientists have insisted that nothing in the universe can go faster than the speed of light, which is 671,232,870 miles per hour. However, even such a seemingly rapid speed is not fast enough for the purposes of the Almighty. Ripping through space at the speed of light, it would still take God over four years to reach Alpha Centauri, the star system nearest ours; over eight and a half years to reach Sirius, the North Star; and over 700 years to reach such bright stars as Canopus, Rigel, and Deneb. These are all within our Milky Way. But there are even more colossal creations farther out.

The scriptures tell us that within such great distances God has much to do: "He comprehendeth all things, and all things are before him, and all things are round about him; and he is above all things, and in all things, and is through all things, and is round about all things, and all things are by him, and of him, even God, forever and ever" (D&C 88:41).

This omnipresence is not accomplished by being "everywhere, but nowhere," as the false sectarian notion teaches, but by actually being able to quickly visit place after place. As Elder James E. Talmage explained, "His powers of transferring Himself from place to place

**ARE THERE MORE STARS IN THE SKY OR SANDS ON THE SHORES?** THE SCRIPTURES
IN SEVERAL PLACES USE PHRASES LIKE "SO MANY AS THE STARS OF THE SKY
IN MULTITUDE, AND AS THE SAND WHICH IS BY THE SEA SHORE INNUMERABLE"
(HEBREWS 11:12). SO HOW MANY GRAINS OF SAND ARE ON THE EARTH?
RESEARCHERS AT THE UNIVERSITY OF HAWAII RECENTLY ESTIMATED THERE ARE
7½ QUINTILLION GRAINS OF SAND—THAT'S 7,500,000,000,000,000,000.
BUT THIS IS EXPONENTIALLY SMALLER IN NUMBER THAN THE NUMBER OF THE
STARS IN THE UNIVERSE. SCIENTISTS ESTIMATE THERE ARE ABOUT 300 BILLION
STARS IN OUR MILKY WAY GALAXY BUT ABOUT A TRILLION GALAXIES IN THE
KNOWN UNIVERSE—AND ELLIPTICAL GALAXIES TEND TO HAVE A LOT MORE STARS
THAN SPIRAL ONES LIKE OURS. THE LATEST ESTIMATE IS THAT THERE ARE 300
SEXTILLION STARS IN THE KNOWN UNIVERSE (SEXTILLION IS A 1 WITH 21 ZEROES).‡

are infinite; plainly, however, His person cannot be in more than one
place at any one time."[76]

Therefore, God, in some marvelous way, has been able to manipulate
the space-time continuum in such a way that He is, in fact, able to "hie
to Kolob / In the twinkling of an eye" and, if He has need, "continue
onward / With that same speed to fly."[77] This method of rapid transit
is certainly also available to the angels. Joseph Smith described one
such ministering servant, the angel Moroni, and how he remarkably
returned to report to the heavens: "After this communication, I saw the
light in the room begin to gather immediately around the person of
him who had been speaking to me, and it continued to do so until the
room was again left dark, except just around him; when instantly I saw,
as it were, a conduit open right up into heaven, and he ascended till he
entirely disappeared" (JS—H 1:43).

---

76 James E. Talmage, *Articles of Faith* (Salt Lake City: Deseret Book, 1899 ), 39.
77 *Hymns*, no. 284.
‡ See Robert Krulwich, "Which Is Greater, The Number Of Sand Grains On Earth
Or Stars In The Sky?" NPR.com, Sep. 17, 2012, http://www.npr.org/blogs/krul-
wich/2012/09/17/161096233/which-is-greater-the-number-of-sand-grains-on-earth-
or-stars-in-the-sky; see also Seth Bornstein, "Number Of Stars In The Universe Could
Be 300 Sextillion, Triple The Amount Scientists Previously Thought: Study," *Huffington
Post*, Dec. 1, 2010, http://www.huffingtonpost.com/2010/12/01/number-of-stars-in-
universe_n_790563.html.

What can travel this interstellar "conduit" at such inconceivable speeds? Anything as small as a child's prayer or as large as the city of Enoch—everything through the will of the Master Scientist is able to shoot through the universe at Godspeed.

## THE SUPREME GOVERNOR OF THE UNIVERSE

As the "supreme Governor of the universe," as He is called in the Bible Dictionary, God is and has to be omnipotent, yet He has a very special connection to us: "Although God created all things and is the ruler of the universe . . . mankind has a special relationship to him that differentiates man from all other created things: man is literally God's offspring, made in his image, whereas all other things are but the work of his hands."[78]

Moroni asked, "Who can comprehend the marvelous works of God?" (Mormon 9:16). Answer: no one can fully comprehend them; however, through engaging ourselves with the scriptures, we have glimpses into the cosmic infrastructure that no one else has ever had.

The Book of Mormon says of a seer that "things shall be made known by them which otherwise could not be known" (Mosiah 8:17). How true this is of Joseph Smith the Prophet and Seer! Though few of us are astronomers or astrophysicists, through studying the Book of Mormon, Doctrine and Covenants, and Pearl of Great Price—all scriptures we have because of Joseph Smith—we may gain understanding of God's universe that Newton, Einstein, or Hawking never had in their lifetimes.

As we study "of things both in heaven and in the earth" (D&C 88:79), we indeed gain an appreciation for the Almighty Father and His Son, the Creator, and His condescension for all. Ironically, as we

---

78 s.v., "God"

search these sometimes-called "deeper" things, the very first principle of the gospel is strengthened, for, as Elder Talmage taught, "Our faith will increase in Him as we learn of Him."[79]

**YODA NOT MODELED AFTER SPENCER W. KIMBALL** WHEN THE *STAR WARS* SEQUEL *THE EMPIRE STRIKES BACK* CAME OUT IN 1980 AND INTRODUCED THE WORLD TO YODA, A RUMOR WAS SPREAD AMONG LATTER-DAY SAINTS THAT HE WAS MODELED AFTER PRESIDENT SPENCER W. KIMBALL. AFTER ALL, THE MORMON PROPHET AND JEDI MASTER ARE BOTH CLEAN-SHAVEN, ELDERLY, HAVE LARGE EARS AND LITTLE BUT WISPY HAIR ON TOP OF THEIR HEADS, POSSESS TREMENDOUS WISDOM, AND SPEAK IN GRAVELY VOICES. "DO . . . OR DO NOT. THERE IS NO TRY," YODA TAUGHT. AND PRESIDENT KIMBALL TAUGHT, "DO IT." SOME EVEN WONDERED IF THERE WERE SHADES OF LDS DOCTRINE INTENTIONALLY LACED THROUGHOUT THE POPULAR SAGA OF LIGHT VERSUS DARKNESS. THE RUMORS BECAME SO PERVASIVE THAT AN EXASPERATED ANNE MERRIFIELD, SECRETARY TO GEORGE LUCAS AT LUCASFILM LTD., FINALLY ISSUED A LETTER: "WE NEVER CEASE TO BE AMAZED AT THE STORIES THAT ARE OUT THERE. YODA WAS MOST DEFINITELY NOT MODELED AFTER SPENCER W. KIMBALL, AND IF PEOPLE BELIEVE THERE IS ANY SORT OF LDS DOCTRINE IN THE 'STAR WARS' MOVIES, IT IS COMPLETELY COINCIDENTAL. THEREFORE, BOTH MYTHS ARE OFFICIALLY DENIED."[‡] THAT SAID, LATTER-DAY SAINT GARY KURTZ, THE PRODUCER OF *STAR WARS* AND *THE EMPIRE STRIKES BACK*, WORKED CLOSELY WITH GEORGE LUCAS ON DEVELOPING THE NATURE OF THE FORCE AND OTHER SPIRITUAL ASPECTS OF THE FILMS. WHILE HIS MORMON BACKGROUND MAY HAVE INFLUENCED THE DISCUSSIONS, KURTZ CLAIMS HIS KNOWLEDGE OF BUDDHISM, HINDUISM, AND NATIVE AMERICAN SPIRITUALITY FROM HIS COLLEGE STUDIES OF COMPARATIVE RELIGIONS IS WHAT REALLY DROVE THE CONVERSATIONS BEHIND THE IDEA OF THE FORCE. [‡‡]

---

79 James E. Talmage, *Articles of Faith* (Salt Lake City: Deseret Book, 1899), 40.

‡ "Yoda Modeled after Mormon Prophet," accessed January 23, 2014, *Mormonmonsters (blog)*, http://mormonmonsters.blogspot.com/2009/09/yoda-modeled-after-mormon-prophet.html.

‡‡ John Baxter, *Mythmaker: The Life and Work of George Lucas* (New York, NY: Avon Books, 1999), 165–66.

## Twelve

# MANLY MEALS

As guys, we love food. After all, the average American male eats over 50 slices of pizza per year, over 100 hamburgers per year, and over 100 pounds of chicken per year. We eat over 5 pounds of chocolate per year, 32 pounds of ice cream, and 32 pounds of cheese. Men eat nearly 60 percent of the food in the world (sorry, ladies). So it's no wonder that we take an interest in the food in the scriptures!

To showcase the wide variety of scriptural foods, let's organize them as a menu. There won't be Moroni macaroni or anything from Mount of Olives Garden here. All are real dishes served up in the scriptures.

## APPETIZERS

### EZEKIEL'S MULTIGRAIN BREAD

Try this heavy homemade favorite as a delicious way to begin your meal! "Take thou also unto thee wheat, and barley, and beans, and lentiles, and millet, and fitches, and put them in one vessel, and make thee bread thereof" (Ezekiel 4:9). The lentils are an especially tasty ingredient, since the Middle Eastern tradition was to grind roasted lentils and press and fry them in oil before putting them in bread or cake (similar to Arab falafel). The "fitches" spoken of in the ingredient list is hulled wheat, also called spelt. "All grain is ordained for the use of man and of beasts, to be the staff of life," the Lord reminded us (D&C 89:14).

> **HUNGER AFTER MORE THAN FOOD** "BLESSED ARE THEY WHICH DO HUNGER AND THIRST AFTER RIGHTEOUSNESS: FOR THEY SHALL BE FILLED."
> **MATTHEW 5:6**

## JACOB'S MESS OF POTTAGE

Many diners prefer to begin their meal with a little soup, and nothing beats this hearty classic! If you're just coming home after a long day in the field, this aromatic red lentil soup is so savory you may be tempted to trade your birthright for it. "And Esau said to Jacob, Feed me, I pray thee, with that same red pottage. . . . Then Jacob gave Esau bread and pottage of lentiles; and he did eat and drink, and rose up, and went his way: thus Esau despised his birthright" (Genesis 25:30, 34).

## GIDEON'S BROTH AND CAKES

Want both bread and broth to start things out? Try Gideon's "unleavened cakes of an ephah of flour." An ephah is a good-sized measurement, showing that these baked goods were made with plenty of flour. Being unleavened, they were flatbread without a rising agent and were especially important to the Jews during Passover meals. Gideon put the finishing touch on his unleavened cakes by setting them on a rock and pouring broth on top of them (Judges 6:19–20).

## DAVID'S GRAIN-AND-VEGETABLE SALAD

Maybe bread and soup's not your thing and you want a salad before dinner. Why don't you try David's salad? When David came to Mahanaim, a man named Shobi brought him some food, including "earthen vessels" filled with "parched corn, and beans, and lentiles, and parched pulse" (2 Samuel 17:28). This scrumptious mix of legumes and grains is high in amino acids and good for the body.

> **DON'T HAVE JUST BREAD!**
> "MAN SHALL NOT LIVE BY BREAD ALONE, BUT BY EVERY WORD THAT PROCEEDETH OUT OF THE MOUTH OF GOD."
> MATTHEW 4:4

## PASSOVER BITTER-HERB SALAD

From the days of the first Passover dinner, the Jews were told "and with bitter herbs they shall eat it" (Exodus 12:8). These bitter herbs were called by the ancients "maror," and the most common types used for Passover meals were horseradish, romaine lettuce, or chazeret (wild lettuce). These lettuces aren't initially bitter but are after the first taste, which is symbolic of the Israelite experience in Egypt. Romans later developed sweeter head lettuce so they could enjoy their Caesar salads.

## DANIEL'S PULSE

Daniel was so fond of the health benefits of pulse that he preferred it over the king's wine and meat in Babylon: "Prove thy servants, I beseech thee, ten days; and let them give us pulse to eat, and water to drink" (Daniel 1:12). Regardless of whether the pulse in Babylon included pinto beans, kidney beans, navy beans, dry peas, lentils, or something else, we do know it worked wonders on Daniel and his friends. "And at the end of ten days their countenances appeared fairer and fatter in flesh than all the children which did eat the portion of the king's meat" (Daniel 1:15). Mmmm. Pulse.

## HEAVENLY QUAIL

Tired of bread, soup, salad, and legumes? Man up with some meat. No, we don't have hot wings for an appetizer here, but we do have some quail. This smaller game bird is so heavenly because it miraculously appeared among the Israelite tents: "That at even the quails came up, and covered the camp" (Exodus 16:13). Quail meat is dark and has a delicate flavor, which makes this a wise choice for those who may find other wild game birds too strong tasting.

# MAIN COURSE

## PRODIGAL SON'S FATTED CALF

Celebrate like the prodigal son has returned home with some tender veal! "And bring hither the fatted calf, and kill it; and let us eat, and be merry" (Luke 15:23). The common family of ancient Israel ate beef on only the rarest of occasions, so it was truly a feast of celebration when they slaughtered the fattened calf. And hey, with veal cutlets, veal parmigiana, fried escalopes, and Austrian Wiener schnitzel, there are sooo many delectable ways to enjoy a fatted calf!

## MANNA FROM HEAVEN

One of the fine vegetarian entrées on today's menu is manna: "And the house of Israel called the name thereof Manna: and it was like coriander seed, white; and the taste of it was like wafers made with honey" (Exodus 16:31). Our manna is gathered from the ground fresh every day: "And they gathered it every morning, every man according to his eating: and when the sun waxed hot, it melted." No leftovers here, since day-old manna "bred worms, and stank" (Exodus 16:20–21). Manna is delicious and sustaining, and Moses called it "the bread which the Lord hath given you to eat" (Exodus 16:15). There are also a variety of ways to serve your manna: "And the people went about, and gathered it, and ground it in mills, or beat it in a mortar, and baked it in pans, and made cakes of it: and the taste of it was as the taste of fresh oil" (Numbers 11:8). Heck, you could eat the stuff for decades! "And the children of Israel did eat manna forty years" (Exodus 16:35).

## NEPHI'S RAW GAME MEAT

If you're tired of ordering manna, you may have fallen into the same trap as the Israelites, where "among them fell a lusting: and the children of Israel also wept again, and said, Who shall give us flesh to eat?" (Numbers 11:4). So for some *real* meat, try some raw game, fresh from Nephi's hunt with his newly made wooden bow: "I did slay wild beasts, insomuch that I did obtain food for our families," Nephi said. "And now when they beheld that I had obtained food, how great was their joy!" (1 Nephi 16:31–32). See? This is good stuff. The principal game animal of the Arabian Peninsula is the Arabian oryx, a medium-sized antelope that has been hunted and devoured for centuries. But Lehi's party enjoyed it raw: "We did live upon raw meat in the wilderness" (1 Nephi 17:2). This raw-meat thing caught on with the Lamanite branch of the family, and generations later, it was still their favorite food: "And many of them did eat nothing save it was raw meat" (Enos 1:20). WARNING: Consuming raw or undercooked meats, poultry, seafood, shellfish, or eggs may increase your risk of food-borne illness.

## MULTIPLYING LOAVES AND FISHES

Have a hearty appetite? How about some multiplying loaves and fishes! While teaching 5,000 people along the shores of the Sea of Galilee, Jesus took "five barley loaves, and two small fishes" and after blessing them, broke them into enough pieces to feed the multitude (John 6:9). Not only did they "eat, and were all filled," but "there was taken up of fragments that remained to them twelve baskets" (Luke 9:17). Although this miracle is listed in all four Gospels, only John gave us the detail that the bread was a barley loaf. As for the fish, the most common fish eaten out of the Sea of Galilee is tilapia, and the species from that lake is known today as St. Peter's fish. It is a light white meat that is fluffy, separates easily from the bone, and (most importantly when you are feeding 5,000) is easy to break up. Enjoy, but if you've found that grain seems to expand to fill your stomach easily, you'd better be extra careful with this entrée!

## REBEKAH'S SAVORY MEAT

The patriarch Isaac loved tenderly cooked meat, and no one prepared it as deliciously as his wife, Rebekah. When Isaac was hankering for this favorite meal right before he died, he sent his son Esau out to hunt for some venison: "And make me savoury meat, such as I love, and bring it to me, that I may eat; that my soul may bless thee before I die." While Esau was hunting, Rebekah told their other son Jacob: "Go now to the flock, and fetch me from thence two good kids of the goats; and I will make them savoury meat for thy father, such as he loveth" (Genesis 27:4, 9). This they did, and the old and blind Isaac thought Jacob's savory goat meat was Esau's savory venison, and in his confusion, Isaac gave Jacob the birthright blessing instead. This biblical episode reveals one of two things—either Isaac was so elderly that on his deathbed he could not discern between goat meat and venison (both of which have strong, gamey flavors), or Rebekah's savory meat dish was so delicious and flavorful it really didn't matter which type of meat was used as the base of this entrée. Either way, if it was Isaac's favorite dish, it could be yours too!

## DINNER OF HERBS WITH LOVE

Another vegetarian entrée option on this menu is a dinner of herbs with a heaping side dish of love! After all, we learn from the scriptures, "Better is a dinner of herbs where love is, than a stalled ox and hatred therewith" (Proverb 15:17). This is really saying something. The herbs in biblical times included favorites such as cumin and black cumin, dill, mint, saffron, thyme, capers, and coriander. The Israelites also enjoyed seasoning with dwarf chicory, hyssop, marjoram, mint, black mustard, and reichardia. It wasn't much of a dinner, but with some love, it could be more satisfying than that "stalled ox" eaten under contentious circumstances. Such beef, fattened and raised in a stall for an eventual feast, led to delectable roasts and sirloin steaks that were prized in the ancient world even more than today. But the herbs may be your better choice. Remember, "all wholesome herbs God hath ordained for the constitution, nature, and use of man" (D&C 89:10).

> **FOOD IS GOOD 7 DAYS A WEEK**
> "GIVE US THIS DAY OUR DAILY BREAD."
> MATTHEW 6:11

## KING SOLOMON'S SAMPLER PLATTER

The daily allowance for the court of King Solomon included "ten fat oxen, and twenty oxen out of the pastures, and an hundred sheep, beside harts, and roebucks, and fallowdeer, and fatted fowl" (1 Kings 4:23). Why taste just one type of meat per night when you can sample half a dozen! The fat oxen are pampered beef, fattened up and grain fed for a flavorful and well-marbled meat. The oxen from the pasture are delicious, free-range beef, giving a wilder grass-fed flavor profile. The lamb and mutton were some of the most common meat enjoyed in ancient Israel and would have been good comfort food and a staple for any royal meal. The variety of venison on Solomon's platter was impressive, including the hart (an old term for a fully matured male deer), the roebuck (the roe deer is a relatively small animal), and the fallow deer (a larger but less muscular deer than the roe). The fatted fowl of Solomon's platter was likely the rich meat of geese. This entrée is ideal for the meat lover in your group! Remember, "flesh also of beasts and of the fowls of the air, I, the Lord, have ordained for the use of man with thanksgiving." But don't eat too much meat because "nevertheless they are to be used sparingly" (D&C 89:12).

## DESSERT

### HOLY LAND BUTTER AND HONEY

Finish your meal with a little butter and honey, perfect for sweetening a roll or crust of bread. Isaiah prophesied of the Messiah, "Butter and honey shall he eat, that he may know to refuse the evil, and choose the good" (Isaiah 7:15). After all, some fresh butter and honey are the epitome of goodness. Besides, if you are living in a "land of milk and honey," you'd be derelict to not have a smackerel of some from time to time! Our butter from the Holy Land is typically churned from fresh goat's milk, and our wonderfully rich, golden honey is not only a natural alternative to white sugar but is also an exceptional treat in the summer and autumn when it has just been harvested and is at its freshest.

### JEREMIAH'S BASKET OF FIGS

A delicious basket of figs is a common Mediterranean treat, and this fruit has been providing sweet flavors and health benefits since

antiquity. After all, we know fig trees were even common in the Garden of Eden because Adam and Eve used fig leaves to cover their nakedness. Figs are among the richest sources of fiber and calcium, but if you order a basket of figs, you want the very good ones: "One basket had very good figs, even like the figs that are first ripe: and the other basket had very naughty figs, which could not be eaten, they were so bad" (Jeremiah 24:2). No one likes naughty figs! Speaking of naughty figs, once, when Jesus was hungry, He came upon a fig tree. Disappointed that the tree had no fruit, He cursed it. The next day, as they walked by the same tree, "Peter calling to remembrance saith unto him, Master, behold, the fig tree which thou cursedst is withered away" (Mark 11:21). Naughty figs!

## DAVID'S FIG CAKE AND RAISINS

Nothing revives your spirits like this cake, a treat prepared in the royal house of King David for an Egyptian guest: "And they gave him a piece of a cake of figs, and two clusters of raisins: and when he had eaten, his spirit came again to him" (1 Samuel 30:12). Figs don't transport well when fresh but make great dried fruit or jams. They are also delicious in pastries, such as in Nabisco's popular Fig Newton or in David's fig cake with raisins.

## JESSE'S CHEESE PLATE

Popular the world over as an after-dinner treat, the rich and varied

flavors and textures of cheese can create a course to remember. When Jesse's sons were with Saul, fighting the Philistines, he sent young David to take them food. But he also gave him some cheese, with a special request: "And carry these ten cheeses unto the captain of their thousand" (1 Samuel 17:18). That's right, Jesse's delicious cheese was an honored gift for the military commander of his sons. This is cheese Jesse likely made himself because we know he had sheep, since David was often their shepherd. There are 82 varieties of strong and bold sheep's-milk cheese. From Abbaye de Belloc to Zamorano cheese, sheep's-milk cheese is known for earthy aromas and savory flavors.

## ELIJAH'S NEVER-ENDING CAKE

Hungry enough for a dessert that never seems to end? Try Elijah's never-ending cake! When Elijah went to the home of the widow of

Zarephath, he asked her to gather her last remaining meal and oil: "And Elijah said unto her, Fear not; go and do as thou hast said: but make me thereof a little cake first, and bring it unto me, and after make for thee and for thy son" (1 Kings 17:13). What should have been their last meal miraculously continued: "And she, and he, and her house, did eat many days" (1 Kings 17:15).

## BROILED FISH AND HONEYCOMB

When you are finally resurrected someday and thrilled to be reunited with your body, what food will you most want? In the case of Jesus, "they gave him a piece of a broiled fish, and of an honeycomb. And he took it, and did eat before them" (Luke 24:42–43). Now, you may question why the dish of broiled fish and honeycomb is in the dessert portion of this menu, but rest  assured the sweet and sticky goodness of fresh honeycomb qualifies. It can be eaten singly as a wafer of sorts, but it is often crushed and spread on something to sweeten it up—usually bread, but why not broiled fish? Fish prepared in the right way is seen all around the world in exotic desserts, such as smoked salmon puffs, trout crepes, sturgeon Rangoon, and a Thai onion fish sticky rice dessert called Khoaw Neiw Moon Bla Hang.

## FRUIT FROM THE SPIES OF MOSES

A refreshing dessert option would be a fruit plate made of the finest pieces obtained by the 12 spies Moses sent to scout out the promised land: "We came unto the land whither thou sentest us, and surely it floweth with milk and honey; and this is the fruit of it," they said. So they "cut down from thence a branch with one cluster of grapes, and they bare it between two upon a staff; and they brought of the pomegranates, and of the figs" (Numbers 13:23, 27). The fig trees in the Holy Land produced two crops per season, and when

eaten fresh, early ripening figs were especially sweet and regarded as a delicacy. The Mediterranean climate and soil of the mountainous areas of Israel were ideal for growing a large variety of grapes. The flavorful pomegranate would certainly add to the grapes and figs for a delectable fruity dessert plate. "All grain is good for the food of man," we are told, "as also the fruit of the vine; that which yieldeth fruit, whether in the ground or above the ground" (D&C 89:16).

**THE FRUIT OF FAITH** "AND BECAUSE OF YOUR DILIGENCE AND YOUR FAITH AND YOUR PATIENCE WITH THE WORD IN NOURISHING IT, THAT IT MAY TAKE ROOT IN YOU, BEHOLD, BY AND BY YE SHALL PLUCK THE FRUIT THEREOF, WHICH IS MOST PRECIOUS, WHICH IS SWEET ABOVE ALL THAT IS SWEET, AND WHICH IS WHITE ABOVE ALL THAT IS WHITE, YEA, AND PURE ABOVE ALL THAT IS PURE; AND YE SHALL FEAST UPON THIS FRUIT EVEN UNTIL YE ARE FILLED, THAT YE HUNGER NOT, NEITHER SHALL YE THIRST."

ALMA 32:42

## TREE OF LIFE FRUIT

There is some notably delicious fruit in the scriptures, beginning

with the tempting fruit of the tree in the Garden of Eden, but Lehi described a different fruit, an especially wonderful fruit, in his vision of the tree of life: "And it came to pass that I did go forth and partake of the fruit thereof; and I beheld that it was most sweet, above all that I ever before tasted." Lehi also described the remarkable color of the fruit: "Yea, and I beheld that the fruit thereof was white, to exceed all the whiteness that I had ever seen." Not only was the fruit sweet and refreshing, but eating it "filled [Lehi's] soul with exceedingly great joy." So of course he wanted to share such an amazing fruit with others. "I began to be desirous that my family should partake of it also; for I knew that it was desirable above all other fruit" (1 Nephi 8:11–12).

So is Lehi's white fruit the ultimate dessert? And is it on *your* menu? Of course it is, because "it is the love of God . . . it is the most desirable above all things . . . and the most joyous to the soul" (1 Nephi 11:22–23). Bon appetite!

As Latter-day guys, we love superheroes. After all, there is a reason the Salt Lake Comic Con in the heart of Mormondom had one of the biggest-ever debuts of its kind! Fortunately for us, the scriptures are filled with superheroes—brave and true men and women whose faith and access to God's power give them seemingly superhuman powers. These are real-life heroes we can look up to, whose faith we can emulate, whose courage we can reach toward. While there are some great wonder women in the scriptures, many of whom are profiled in another chapter, below are men who could easily be called super.

## RIGHTEOUS WARRIORS OF TRUTH AND JUSTICE

This class of scriptural superheroes is the group anyone would want with them in a fight. They demonstrated such superhuman faith, skill, and strength that the forces of evil shuddered.

**CAPTAIN MORONI**—Forget Captain America; we have Captain Moroni. This hero was brave, loyal, and strategic. His leadership turned the tide for a vastly outnumbered Nephite army and subdued the enemy: "Moroni was a strong and mighty man; he was a man of a perfect understanding," the historian-general Mormon said of him. "Yea, he was a man who was firm in the faith of Christ . . . . Yea, verily, verily I say unto you, if all men had been, and were, and ever

would be, like unto Moroni, behold the very powers of hell would have been shaken forever; yea, the devil would never have power over the hearts of the children of men" (Alma 48:11, 13, 17).

**SUPER-STRONG SAMSON**—Who needs the drama of the Hulk when we have Samson, who had super strength like no one else in the scriptures: "And when he came unto Lehi, the Philistines shouted against him: and the Spirit of the Lord came mightily upon him, and the cords that were upon his arms became as flax that was burnt with fire, and his bands loosed from off his hands." And who needs Thor's hammer Mjölnir when Samson's got the jawbone of an ass? "And he found a new jawbone of an ass, and put forth his hand, and took it, and slew a thousand men therewith. And Samson said, With the jawbone of an ass, heaps upon heaps, with the jaw of an ass have I slain a thousand men" (Judges 15:14–16). Unfortunately, Samson also had his kryptonite: "If I be shaven, then my strength will go from me, and I shall become weak, and be like any other man" (Judges 16:17).

**TEANCUM, JAVELIN THROWER, STEALTH ASSASSIN**—Marvel Comics has Javelin, but the Book of Mormon has Teancum, a real-life freedom fighter who has exceptional skills with the javelin. Teancum "fought valiantly for his country, yea, a true friend to liberty" (Alma 62:37). Not only was he a brave military commander, but Teancum was also as stealthy as Batman sneaking up on the bad guys in the dark. He took out the evil Amalickiah this way: "And it came to pass that Teancum stole privily into the tent of the king, and put a javelin to his heart; and he did cause the death of the king immediately that he did not awake his servants" (Alma 51:34). But when he also eliminated Amalickiah's brother and successor, Ammoron, Teancum lost his own life before he could escape: "Teancum in his anger did go forth into the camp of the Lamanites, and did let himself down over the walls of the city. And he went forth with a cord, from place to place, insomuch that he did find the king; and he did cast a javelin at him, which did pierce him near the heart. But behold, the king did awaken his servants before he died, insomuch that they did pursue Teancum, and slew him" (Alma 62:36). Still, this superhero single-handedly took out the Nephite nation's two worst enemies!

**AMMON, SUPER-SERVANT ARM SLICER**—Not only is Ammon as loyal to King Lamoni as Batman is to Commissioner Gordon, but he also has the ability to use a sword with the deadly accuracy of superhero Blade using his two-edged sword or Electra using her three-pronged ninja Sais: "But behold, every man that lifted his club to smite Ammon, he smote off their arms with his sword; for he did withstand their blows by smiting their arms with the edge of his sword, insomuch that they began to be astonished, and began to flee before him; yea, and they were not few in number; and he caused them to flee by the strength of his arm" (Alma 17:37). Less celebrated but equally as effective as Ammon's swordsmanship is his use of the sling: "Ammon stood forth and began to cast stones at them with his sling; yea, with mighty power he did sling stones amongst them; and thus he slew a certain number of them insomuch that they began to be astonished at his power" (Alma 17:36).

**LDS SUPERHERO COMIC BOOK?** ARTIST CHRIS HOFFMAN LAUNCHED A COMIC BOOK IN 2013 FEATURING AN ALL-**LDS** SUPERHERO TEAM. SALT CITY STRANGERS FEATURES SON OF BIGFOOT, THE GULL, DEPUTY DESERET, DEN MOTHER, AND GOLDEN SPIKE. "UTAH AND MEMBERS OF THE CHURCH DON'T GET A FAIR SHAKE IN MODERN COMIC BOOKS," HOFFMAN SAID. "GODZILLA WAS HERE ONCE, TEARING DOWN THE CHURCH OFFICE BUILDING. ONE OF SHE HULK'S SECRETARIES IN HER OFFICE IS **LDS**."‡

**ADAM/MICHAEL, ARCHANGEL AND DRAGON FIGHTER**—Clark Kent is really Superman, Bruce Wayne is really Batman, Peter Parker is really Spider-Man, and we learn from Latter-day revelation the secret identity of our forefather Adam: "And they rose up and blessed

---

‡ Bryan Schott, "LDS Superheroes Take On Utah Stereotypes in New Comic Book," *City Weekly*, May 24, 2013.

Adam, and called him Michael, the prince, the archangel" (D&C 107:54). And just as Wonder Woman can use her Lasso of Truth to unveil what's really going on, Michael's abilities include revealing the true nature of evil, such as when he appeared "on the banks of the Susquehanna, detecting the devil when he appeared as an angel of light" (D&C 128:20), or rebuking the devil as "he disputed about the body of Moses" (Jude 1:9). This heroic archangel has been battling Lucifer successfully since the preexistence: "And there was war in heaven; Michael and his angels fought against the dragon; and the dragon and his angels fought against Michael. And the dragon prevailed not against Michael" (JST, Revelation 12:6–7). And in "the battle of the great God" that will occur after the millennium, Satan and the armies of hell will lose once more, "for Michael shall fight their battles, and shall overcome him" (D&C 88:115).

**DAVID THE GIANT SLAYER—**
Whether it's the Incredible Hulk fighting the Abomination or Thor defeating the frost giants, real superheroes know how to take down giants. While Saul and his armies cowered from the giant Goliath of Gath, the young shepherd David came on the scene filled with superhuman faith and confidence: "Who is this uncircumcised Philistine, that he

should defy the armies of the living God?" David asked. "And David said to Saul, Let no man's heart fail because of him; thy servant will go and fight with this Philistine" (1 Samuel 17:26, 32). David was not shy, either, in acknowledging where his strength came from: "Thou comest to me with a sword, and with a spear, and with a shield: but I come to thee in the name of the Lord of hosts, the God of the armies of Israel,

whom thou hast defied" (1 Samuel 17:45). In his first shot with the
sling, David landed a smooth stone deep into the forehead of Goliath
with superhuman accuracy, causing the big man to fall on his face. He
then unsheathed Goliath's own sword "and cut off his head therewith.
And when the Philistines saw their champion was dead, they fled" (1
Samuel 17:51).

## REMARKABLE PRIESTS & PROPHETS

This group may not have quite the omniscience of Infinity or the
Phantom Stranger, but their spiritual sensitivities give them better vision
than Doctor Mid-Nite. They are heroes who magnify their assignments
and missions better than any member of the Justice League.

**MIGHTY FAITHFUL MELCHIZEDEK**—When Melchizedek became
king in the land of Salem, "his people had waxed strong in iniquity
and abomination; yea, they had all gone astray; they were full of all
manner of wickedness." But no worries, Melchizedek whipped them
into shape. He "exercised mighty faith," blessed their lives with the
priesthood, and preached repentance. "And behold, they did repent;
and Melchizedek did establish peace in the land in his days; therefore
he was called the prince of peace." Alma the Younger was impressed
with this amazing high priest and wrote, "Now, there were many
before him, and also there were many afterwards, but none were
greater" (Alma 13:17–19).

**JOHN THE BAPTIST**—The greatest compliment anyone can have
is from Jesus Himself, who said: "A prophet? yea, I say unto you,
and more than a prophet. . . . Among them that are born of women
there hath not risen a greater than John the Baptist" (Matthew 11:9,
11). Superheroes have their distinctive uniforms, and John was no
exception: "And John was clothed with camel's hair, and with a girdle
of a skin about his loins; and he did eat locusts and wild honey"
(Mark 1:6). Jesus said it was intentional that John was not "a man
clothed in soft raiment" (Matthew 11:8). After all, his superhero
outfit had to fit the part of "the voice of one crying in the wilderness,
Prepare ye the way of the Lord, make his paths straight" (Mark 1:3).

In addition to preparing the world for the ministry of the Messiah, John baptized Jesus and could not be stopped from advancing the work of the Aaronic Priesthood. Even once Herod Antipas beheaded him, his work was not stopped. Like DC Comic's Resurrection Man or Marvel's Mister Immortal, death could not halt the work of this hero! On May 15, 1829, John the Baptist "descended in a cloud of light" and conferred the Aaronic Priesthood on the heads of Joseph Smith and Oliver Cowdery (JS—H 1:68 and D&C 13:1).

**JOSEPH SMITH: SUPER SEER**—Cypher and Wonder Woman (and C-3PO, for that matter) can understand various languages, and from time to time in the scriptures, seers have had this super-ability. In these cases, seers, whether Mosiah or Joseph Smith, used the Urim and Thummim, or seer stones, to interpret languages and translate records.

The Prophet Joseph was phenomenal: "Joseph Smith, the Prophet and Seer of the Lord, has done more, save Jesus only, for the salvation of men in this world, than any other man that ever lived in it," John Taylor, then a member of the Quorum of the Twelve, wrote. As a seer, Joseph "brought forth the Book of Mormon, which he translated by the gift and power of God," as well as "brought forth the revelations and commandments which compose this book of Doctrine and Covenants, and many other wise documents and instructions for the benefit of the children of men" (D&C 135:3). Thanks to this super seer, Latter-day Saints enjoy some 900 pages of additional scripture. "Praise to the Man who communed with Jehovah! / Jesus anointed that Prophet and Seer / . . . . Death cannot conquer the hero again."[80]

**NEPHI: SHOCKINGLY STRONG**—Havok, a member of the X-Men, can raise his arm and send a shock of energy outward in his defense, but can he also build a ship? Nephi could do both! When those whining older brothers Laman and Lemuel were giving Nephi guff about building the ship, the Lord commanded Nephi, "Stretch forth thine hand again unto thy brethren,

80 *Hymns*, no. 27.

and they shall not wither before thee, but I will shock them, saith the Lord, and this will I do, that they may know that I am the Lord their God." So Nephi did, and "the Lord did shake them." After they fell to the ground from the pulse of energy that emanated from their brother's arm, Laman and Lemuel said, "We know of a surety that the Lord is with thee, for we know that it is the power of the Lord that has shaken us" (1 Nephi 17:53–55).

## POWERFULLY PROTECTED

Some superheroes have special abilities to help them fight, and others have special abilities to defend and protect. Like Captain America's shield and Iron Man's body armor, the protection afforded these heroes is remarkable!

**SAMUEL THE LAMANITE, DIVINELY DEFENDED**—Samuel the Lamanite prophet was better protected than Unus the Untouchable from the *X-Men* comic books. While preaching atop a wall, Samuel's detractors could not harm him: "And they cast stones at him upon the wall, and also many shot arrows at him as he stood upon the wall; but the Spirit of the Lord was with him,  insomuch that they could not hit him with their stones neither with their arrows." Such divine defense had conversion consequences! "Now when they saw that they could not hit him, there were many more who did believe on his words" (Helaman 16:2–3).

**ARMY OF HELAMAN, DEFYING DEATH**—As director of S.H.I.E.L.D., Nick Fury worried about his troops and was pleased when his Avengers saved the day once more without any of them being killed. Similarly, in the Book of Mormon, General Helaman was pleased with his "little band of two thousand and sixty," as he called the young stripling warriors who "fought most desperately," "firm and undaunted," "and did administer death unto all those who opposed them." These young warriors' secret weapon was that "they did obey and observe to perform every word of command with exactness; yea, and even according to their faith it was done unto them; and I did remember the words which they said unto me that their mothers had taught them" (Alma 57:19–21).

And when the fierce battle was over, Helaman wrote, "According to the goodness of God, and to our great astonishment, and also the joy of our whole army, there was not one soul of them who did perish; yea, and neither was there one soul among them who had not received many wounds." Where did this super protective power come from? Helaman explains, "And we do justly ascribe it to the miraculous power of God, because of their exceeding faith in that which they had been taught to believe—that there was a just God, and whosoever did not doubt, that they should be preserved by his marvelous power." Then Helaman, like a proud father, wrote, "Now this was the faith of these of whom I have spoken; they are young, and their minds are firm, and they do put their trust in God continually" (Alma 57:25–27).

**DANIEL THE LION TAMER**—After being tricked into signing an irrevocable royal edict punishing all who prayed by casting them into a den of lions, King Darius was aghast when Daniel, his chief counselor, was brought before him as a violator: "And they brought Daniel, and cast him into the den of lions. Now the king spake and said unto Daniel, Thy God whom thou servest continually, he will  deliver thee." The pained king's faith was sobering. These lions were ferocious when others had  been sent to the den, "the lions had the mastery of them, and brake all their bones in pieces" (Daniel 6:16–24).

After a sleepless night, Darius returned to the den and hollered down, "O Daniel, servant of the living God, is thy God, whom thou servest continually, able to deliver thee from the lions?" To his delight, he heard the reply, "O king, live for ever. My God hath sent his angel, and hath shut the lions' mouths." Divine protection had enveloped Daniel, and the super faith of both him and his friend the king invested him with safety. "So Daniel was taken up out of the den, and no manner of hurt was found upon him, because he believed in his God" (Daniel 6:20–23).

**JOHN TAYLOR AND WILLARD RICHARDS**—They may not have had the impervious skin of superhero Luke Cage, but Apostles John Taylor and Willard Richards had some amazing divine protection while bullets flew around them in Carthage Jail. Elder Taylor wrote of the incident in Carthage, Illinois, on June 27, 1844, that resulted in the deaths of the Prophet Joseph Smith and his brother Patriarch Hyrum Smith: "John Taylor and Willard Richards, two of the Twelve, were the only persons in the room at the time; the former was wounded in a savage manner with four balls, but has since recovered; the latter, through the providence of God, escaped, without even a hole in his robe" (D&C 135:2).

During the raid on the jail, the crystal of Elder Taylor's pocket watch stopped a shot aimed for his heart. "I felt that the Lord had preserved me by a special act of mercy," John Taylor said of the stopped bullet, "that my time had not yet come, and that I had still a work to perform upon the earth."[81]

As for his colleague, "Dr. Richards' escape was miraculous; he being a very large man, and in the midst of a shower of balls, yet he stood unscathed, with the exception of a ball which grazed the tip end of the lower part of his left ear."[82] His escape fulfilled literally a prophecy which Joseph made over a year previously, that the time would come that the balls would fly around him like hail, and he should see his friends fall on the right and on the left, but that there should not be a hole in his garment.

---

81 Brigham H. Roberts, *Life of John Taylor* (Salt Lake City: George Q. Cannon & Sons Co., 1892), 150.

82 *HC*, 6:619.

## SHADRACH, MESHACH, AND ABED-NEGO: THE TRIO WHO WOULD NOT BURN

—Because Shadrach, Meshach, and Abed-nego would not worship his idol, King Nebuchadnezzar, in his fury, had the three young Jews thrown into a fiery furnace: the king "commanded that they should heat the furnace one seven times more than it was wont to be heated." The furnace was cranked up, and the heat roaring out of it was so intense that the mighty men of Babylon who threw the prisoners into it were themselves consumed. But the king was flabbergasted when he looked into the furnace: "Lo, I see four men loose, walking in the midst of the fire, and they have no hurt; and the form of the fourth is like the Son of God." These four were more flame resistant than the Fantastic Four! Nebuchadnezzar called for them to come out of the fire, which they did. Although they were expecting something like the Human Torch, all the royal courtiers "saw these men, upon whose bodies the fire had no power, nor was an hair of their head singed, neither were their coats changed, nor the smell of fire had passed on them." These men had the faith and divine protection to stop Pyro or any other flaming enemy. "Then Nebuchadnezzar spake, and said, Blessed be the God of Shadrach, Meshach, and Abed-nego, who hath sent his angel, and delivered his servants that trusted in him" (Daniel 3:19–28).

## NOAH: PROTECTED FROM FLOODWATERS

—Some superheroes can withstand flames, others lions, but Noah overcame a catastrophic flood! He was obedient enough to build an ark, as the Lord commanded, to survive the mighty rains that came and save his family and a few favorite pets while he was at it. "Noah was a just man and perfect in his generations," Moses described him. "And Noah walked with God" (Genesis 6:9). And like Clark Kent, Adam, and others, Noah had his secret identity. Joseph Smith taught that Noah was really the angel Gabriel and was second only to Adam in the hierarchy of angels in holding the keys of salvation.[83] Gabriel was the angel who announced the births of John the Baptist and Jesus and ministered in other capacities as well.

## SUPERHEROES DOING SUPER THINGS

**JOSEPH: DREAMER OF EGYPT**—Dream Girl (also known as Nura Nal) can see the future in dreams, as can the supervillain Destiny. But their superhero outfits don't hold a candle to Joseph's technicolor dream coat! "Can we find such a one as this is, a man in whom the Spirit of God is?" Pharaoh exclaimed after witnessing Joseph interpret his dreams. "And Pharaoh said unto Joseph, Forasmuch as God hath shewed thee all this, there is none so discreet and wise as thou art" (Genesis 41:38–39).

**PETER: WATER WALKER**—To walk on water would be a super-feat indeed, and one Peter mastered—almost: "And when Peter was come down out of the ship, he walked on the water, to go to Jesus" (Matthew 14:29). But when the wind and waves kicked up, Peter's confidence began to wane, and he began to sink and required the help of the Master to finish. Still, even attempting to walk on water with any degree of success would require super faith.

**BROTHER OF JARED: MOUNTAIN MOVER**—In the superhero world, heroines like Petra and Terra can move rocks, mud, and earth. In the scriptures, though, the brother of Jared could move mountains! "For the brother of Jared said unto the mountain Zerin, Remove— and it was removed," Moroni recalled. "And if he had not had faith it would not have moved; wherefore [the Lord worketh] after men have faith" (Ether 12:30). No matter how you look at it, Mahonri Moriancumr's mountain-moving faith was phenomenal!

**JONAH: A REAL AQUAMAN**—Aquaman can swim to the depths of the oceans and be one with the seas, but Jonah truly survived three days in the deep

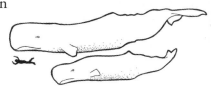

**WHAT KIND OF FISH SWALLOWED JONAH?** THE LARGEST FISH IN THE STRICT SENSE IS A GREAT WHITE SHARK, WHICH CAN EXCEED 20 FEET IN LENGTH AND DOES INHABIT THE MEDITERRANEAN. THE PROBLEM WITH JAWS BEING JONAH'S GREAT FISH IS THAT IT CANNOT SWALLOW A HUMAN WHOLE. TODAY WE KNOW THAT WHALES ARE MAMMALS, BUT THE ANCIENTS SIMPLY CLASSED THEM ALL AS "GREAT FISH," SO IT WAS LIKELY A WHALE THAT SWALLOWED JONAH. THE PROBLEM WITH THE LARGEST WHALE—THE BLUE WHALE, SOMETIMES 98 FEET IN LENGTH—IS THAT IT IS NOT FOUND IN THE MEDITERRANEAN AND, LIKE ALL BALEEN WHALES (THAT EAT KRILL), IT WOULD CHOKE ON ANYTHING LARGER THAN A HERRING.

THE "GREAT FISH" FROM JONAH'S WHALE OF A TALE WAS LIKELY A SPERM WHALE. FOUND IN THE MEDITERRANEAN SEA, SPERM WHALES LOVE ICE-FREE WATERS AT LEAST 3,300 FEET DEEP. THERE WERE PLENTY OF THESE DEEP POCKETS ALONG JONAH'S ESCAPE ROUTE WEST BETWEEN JOPPA AND TARSHISH. ADULT MALES TYPICALLY GROW TO 67 FEET IN LENGTH, AND SOME REPORTEDLY HIT 80 FEET. THEY FEAST ON ANIMALS MUCH LARGER THAN HUMANS, PRIMARILY GIANT AND COLOSSAL SQUIDS, AND COULD HAVE EASILY SWALLOWED JONAH WHOLE. THEY HAVE A SLOW DIGESTIVE TRACT, INCLUDING THE LONGEST INTESTINAL SYSTEM IN THE WORLD, SO JONAH COULD HAVE HUNG OUT IN THE STOMACH OF THE BEAST FOR 3 MISERABLE DAYS AND NIGHTS IN WHAT HE DESCRIBED AS "THE BELLY OF HELL" (JONAH 2:2).

SPERM WHALES ARE THE DEEPEST-DIVING MAMMAL (PLUNGING UP TO 9,800 FEET FOR PREY). WHEN JONAH PRAYED IN THE BELLY OF THE BEAST AND SAID, "THE WATERS COMPASSED ME ABOUT, EVEN TO THE SOUL: THE DEPTH CLOSED ME ROUND ABOUT" (JONAH 2:5), HE WAS NOT EXAGGERATING!

REMARKABLY, SPERM WHALES HAVE THE LARGEST BRAIN OF ANY ANIMAL ON EARTH (5 TIMES HEAVIER THAN A HUMAN'S), SO, UNLIKE JONAH, THE WHALE PROMPTLY OBEYED GOD: "AND THE LORD SPAKE UNTO THE FISH, AND IT VOMITED OUT JONAH UPON THE DRY LAND" (JONAH 2:10). THE CLICKING VOCALIZATION OF THE SPERM WHALE IS THE LOUDEST SOUND MADE BY ANY ANIMAL ON EARTH (230 DECIBELS UNDERWATER, WHICH IS AS LOUD AS 1,000 TONS OF TNT EXPLODING). SURELY THE WHALE USED THIS AMAZINGLY NOISY FORM OF ECHOLOCATION AND INTERSPECIES COMMUNICATION NUMEROUS TIMES IN THE 3 DAYS WITH JONAH, ADDING EXTRA MEANING TO THE VERSES: "THEN JONAH PRAYED UNTO THE LORD HIS GOD OUT OF THE FISH'S BELLY, AND SAID, I CRIED BY REASON OF MINE AFFLICTION UNTO THE LORD, AND HE HEARD ME; OUT OF THE BELLY OF HELL CRIED I, AND THOU HEARDEST MY VOICE" (JONAH 2:1-2).

after being tossed overboard and swallowed by a great fish. And if his "great fish" was actually a sperm whale, which it likely was, he could have plunged deeper in the Mediterranean than Aquaman would dare! The sperm whale is the deepest-diving mammal, swimming nearly 10,000 feet below the water's surface.

**PRISON-BREAKING DUOS**—Batman has Robin, Captain America has Bucky, and Superman has Jimmy Olsen at the *Daily Planet*. Sometimes the best superheroes operate with a sidekick, and that's certainly true for a few pairs of scriptural prison breakers. We have Alma the Younger and Amulek, who, while in prison, prayed, "O Lord, give us strength according to our faith which is in Christ, even unto deliverance." The resulting earthquake destroyed the prison walls and killed their captors, "and they were loosed from their bands; and the prison had fallen to the earth" (Alma 14:26, 28). Then we have Paul and Silas, who also "prayed, and sang praises unto God: and the prisoners heard them. And suddenly there was a great earthquake, so that the foundations of the prison were shaken: and immediately all the doors were opened, and every one's bands were loosed" (Acts 16:25–26).

But most remarkable of the prison-breaking duos are the brothers Nephi and Lehi, sons of Helaman and missionary companions. After being thrown into the Lamanite prison, they too prayed for deliverance. And "they were encircled about with a pillar of fire, and that it burned them not," which dumbfounded their captors. Then a dark cloud descended on the prison, and the walls shook. Three times a voice from the heavens called the prison keepers to repentance, and finally they turned to God. The dark cloud disappeared, and "they saw the heavens open; and angels came down out of heaven and ministered unto them" (Helaman 5:21–48).

**MOSES AND AARON: MEN OF THE STAFF**—The Green Lantern has his power ring, Thor has his hammer, and Moses and Aaron have their rods. Moses took his rod and "cast it on the ground, and it became a serpent." When he picked it up by the tail, it once again became a rod (Exodus 4:3). Very cool. Aaron also turned his rod into a serpent in Pharaoh's court, and when Pharaoh's sorcerers also turned their rods into snakes, "Aaron's rod swallowed up their rods" (Exodus 7:12). Later, Aaron "lifted up the rod, and smote the waters that were in the river . . . and all the waters that were in the river were turned to blood" (Exodus 7:20). Aaron stretched out his rod on other occasions to generate frogs, lice, and other plagues to help persuade Pharaoh to let the Israelites leave Egypt, and once on their way, it was Moses's rod that stretched over the waters of the Red Sea to part a path for them to escape. "And the children of Israel went into the midst of the sea upon the dry ground" (Exodus 14:22). In the wilderness, the Lord commanded Moses to use this same super rod to "smite the rock, and there shall come water out of it, that the people may drink. And Moses did so" (Exodus 17:6).

## IN A CLASS BY HIMSELF

The greatest superhero of all, of course, is our Savior Jesus Christ. What other hero has ever saved all of humanity from the finality of the grave? Because of Him, we will all be resurrected someday. Oh, death, where is thy sting? What other hero has ever suffered so much so all of us have a path, if we accept it, back to our Father's presence? Happily-ever-afters are only possible because of our Redeemer, who overcame sin. The Conqueror of Death and Hell is surely in a class by Himself.

"None other has had so profound an influence upon all who have lived and will yet live upon the earth," the First Presidency and Twelve declared in "The Living Christ: The Testimony of the Apostles," a special declaration issued in commemoration of Christ's 2,000th birthday. "He was the Great Jehovah of the Old Testament, the Messiah of the New." Indeed, Christ is the ultimate hero of the scriptures.

So, despite the fun facts, interesting tidbits, and curious stories and characters of the scriptures, let us never forget the primary purpose of God's holy words: "And we talk of Christ, we rejoice in Christ, we preach of Christ, we prophesy of Christ, and we write according to our prophecies," Nephi said, "that our children may know to what source they may look for a remission of their sins" (2 Nephi 25:26).

Jesus is the Christ. He is absolutely the hero of the scriptures and of our lives. Because of Him we can look to the reality of "the blessed and happy state of those that keep the commandments of God. For behold, they are blessed in all things, both temporal and spiritual; and if they hold out faithful to the end they are received into heaven, that thereby they may dwell with God in a state of never-ending happiness" (Mosiah 2:41).

## SUPERMAN'S DIVINE SIMILARITIES

"SUPERMAN'S STORY GOES SOMETHING LIKE THIS. . . . FROM ABOVE, A HEAVENLY FATHER SENDS HIS ONLY SON TO SAVE THE EARTH. WHEN THE SON COMES DOWN TO EARTH, HE'LL BE RAISED BY TWO PARENTS WHO ORIGINALLY HAD THE NAMES MARY AND JOSEPH—NOW THIS IS THE SUPERMAN STORY WE ARE TALKING ABOUT," STEPHEN SKELTON, AUTHOR OF *THE GOSPEL ACCORDING TO THE WORLD'S GREATEST SUPERHERO*, EXPLAINS. SIMILAR TO CHRIST'S SPENDING TIME IN THE WILDERNESS BEFORE BEGINNING HIS MINISTRY, SUPERMAN GOES TO THE ARCTIC TO COMMUNE WITH HIS FATHER'S SPIRIT. "AT AGE 30, SUPERMAN WILL EMBARK ON HIS PUBLIC MISSION—THIS IS THE SAME AGE AS CHRIST," HE EXPLAINS. "AND THEN SUPERMAN WILL, IN HIS MISSION AND MINISTRY, FIGHT FOR TRUTH AND JUSTICE, 2 FUNDAMENTAL, BIBLICAL PRINCIPLES TO BASE A MISSION ON." IRONICALLY, TWO JEWISH TEENAGERS, JERRY SIEGEL AND JOEL SHUSTER, BEGAN THE SUPERMAN FRANCHISE IN THE 1930s AND ORIGINALLY WANTED TO CRAFT A SUPERHERO AROUND THE STRENGTH OF SAMSON.‡

These scriptures are the roadmap to following His life, example, and commandments. Keep them as part of *your* life! "Search the scriptures," the Master lovingly encourages, "for in them ye think ye have eternal life: and they are they which testify of me" (John 5:39).

‡ Hannah Goodwyn, "Superman and Jesus: Superman's Origin and Parallels to Jesus, Christian Broadcasting Network, accessed January 27, 2014, https://www.cbn.com/entertainment/screen/superman-gospel-story.aspx.

## Art Credits

Page 1: *LDS Standard Works.* Courtesy of Wikimedia Commons; for more information, visit www.commons.wikimedia.org.

Page 2: *Man and Scriptures* by Jayme Asbell-Luckau.

Page 2: *Scripture.* Courtesy of Wikimedia Commons; for more information, visit www.commons.wikimedia.org.

Page 6: *Carpentry Tools from the Shipwreck of the* Mary Rose. Courtesy of Wikimedia Commons; for more information, visit www.commons.wikimedia.org.

Page 6: *Old Siberian Mallet.* Courtesy of Wikimedia Commons; for more information, visit www.commons.wikimedia.org.

Page 6: Modified image by Mike Winder, based on *Jesus Working in Joseph's Carpenter Shop* by Del Parson.

Page 7: *Ancient Greek Chariot* by Alexander Yakovlev, 1911. Courtesy of Wikimedia Commons; for more information, visit www.commons.wikimedia.org.

Page 7: Egyptian Chariot from *Nineveh and Its Palaces* by Joseph Bonomi, 1853. Courtesy of Wikimedia Commons; for more information, visit www.commons.wikimedia.org.

Page 9: *Liahona* by Jayme Asbell-Luckau.

Page 10: *High Priest and Priests.* Courtesy of Wikimedia Commons; for more information, visit www.commons.wikimedia.org.

Page 11: *Urim and Thummim.* Courtesy of Wikimedia Commons; for more information, visit www.commons.wikimedia.org.

Page 13: Michael Ward image, free for public use with GNU General Public License, modified by Mike Winder.

Page 14: *Solomon's Temple.* Courtesy of Wikimedia Commons; for more information, visit www.commons.wikimedia.org.

Page 15: *King Herod.* Licensed under royalty-free license from supercoloring.com.

Page 17: *Tulum, Mexico.* Courtesy of Wikimedia Commons; for more information, visit www.commons.wikimedia.org.

Page 19: *Skyscraper Proximity* by Mike Winder.

Page 20: *Skyscraper Comparison* by Jayme Asbell-Luckau.

Page 23: *Samson and Delilah* by Gerrit van Honthorst, 1615, Museum of Art, Cleveland, Ohio.

Page 23: *The Day Dream* by Dante Gabriel Rossetti, 1880. Victoria and Albert Museum, London.

Page 24: *Dante's Vision of Rachel and Leah* by Dante Gabriel Rossetti, 1855. Tate Gallery, London.

Page 24: Section of *Bathsheba at Her Bath* by Rembrandt, 1654. Louvre, Paris.

Page 25: *Rebecca and Eliezer* by Bartolomé Esteban Murillo, 1652. Prado, Madrid.

Page 25: Modified section of *Adam and Eve in Paradise* by Jan Gossaert, 1525. Gemäldegaleiie, Berlin.

Page 26: *Ruth in Boaz's Field* by Julius Schnorr von Carolsfeld, 1828. National Gallery, London.

Page 26: *Woman Holding a Sistrum*, Egyptian, 1250–1200 B.C. Walters Art Museum, Baltimore, Maryland.

Page 27: *The Meeting of Jacob and Rachel* by William Dyce, 1850. Royal Academy, London.

Page 28: *Queen Esther* by Minerva Teichert, 1937. Brigham Young Museum of Art, Provo, Utah.

Page 31: *Boat Comparison* by Jayme Asbell-Luckau.

Page 33: *Camel.* Courtesy of Wikimedia Commons; for more information, visit www.commons.wikimedia.org.

Page 36: *Olmec head.* Courtesy of Wikimedia Commons; for more information, visit www.commons.wikimedia.org.

Page 37: *Reed Ship.* Courtesy of Wikimedia Commons; for more information, visit www.commons.wikimedia.org.

Page 39: *Phoenician Ship.* Courtesy of Wikimedia Commons; for more information, visit www.commons.wikimedia.org.

Page 40: *The Kingdom of David and Solomon.* Freely distributed through bible-history.com.

Page 41: *Jonah's Ship in the Storm* by Caspar Luiken, 1712, from "Historiae celebriores Veteris Testamenti Iconibus representatae."

Page 42: Map by Mike Winder.

Page 45: *Fisherman on the Sea of the Galilee,* between 1890 and 1905. Commercial royalty-free license, for more information, visit http://imageenvision.com/info/license_commercial.html.

Page 48: *Gladius.* Courtesy of Wikimedia Commons; for more information, visit www.commons.wikimedia.org.

Page 49: *David and Ahimelech,* by David Martin, 1639-1721, from "Historie des Ouden en Nieuwen Testaments : verrykt met meer dan vierhonderd printverbeeldingen in koper gesneeden."

Page 49: *Sling and stones.* Courtesy of Wikimedia Commons; for more information, visit www.commons.wikimedia.org.

Page 50: *How to throw a sling* by Jayme Asbell-Luckau.

Page 51: *Floating ax* by Jayme Asbell-Luckau.

Page 52: Illustration from the Tovar Codex, Museo Nacional de Antropología, Mexico City.

Page 52: *Five Ancient Swords* by Jayme Asbell-Luckau.

Page 53: *Sword of St. Peter, Poznań Archdioecesial Museum.* Courtesy of Wikimedia Commons; for more information, visit www.commons.wikimedia.org.

Page 55: Illustration from the Tovar Codex, Museo Nacional de Antropología, Mexico City.

Page 56: *Ark of the Covenant* by Jayme Asbell-Luckau.

Page 57: Section of illustration for the Indiana Jones Bible, by Ralph McQuarrie.

Page 59: *Witch Legs Halloween Craft.* freeware courtesy allyou.com.

Page 60: *Selling Dead Meat to Aliens* by Jayme Asbell-Luckau.

Page 61: *Elisha Avenged by She Bears*, unknown artist, woodcut, modified by Mike Winder.

Page 63: *Long/Man, Short Bed* by Jayme Asbell-Luckau.

Page 63: *Christmas Tree,* freeware courtesy bestdesignplan.com.

Page 64: *A Flying Roll* by Jayme Asbell-Luckau.

Page 71: *Olmec Warrior*, bronze sculpture by Milo, unknown date.

Page 72: *Carthaginian War Elephants Engage Roman Infantry at the Battle of Zama (202 BC)* by Henri-Paul Motte, 1890.

Page 74: *General Joseph Smith's Last Address*, lithographic print by John Hafen, 1888.

Page 76: *Abijah Leads Judah to Battle.* Courtesy of Wikimedia Commons; for more information, visit www.commons.wikimedia.org.

Page 78: *Hill Cumorah* by George E. Anderson, 1907.

Page 81: *Tiglath-Pileser III Besieging a Town, from Nineveh*, unknown Assyrian artist. British Museum, London.

Page 82: From *Nineveh and Its Remains* by Austen Henry Layard, 1849. London.

Page 83: *Judeo-Israelite War* by Isaac-Louis Le Maistre de Sacy, 1613–1684. Paris.

Page 84: *Stamp Seal Inscribed, Hebrew, Human Image*, Israel Antiquities Authority.

Page 88: *Height Comparisons* by Jayme Asbell-Luckau.

Page 89: *Bust of Methuselah.* Creation Museum, Petersburg, Kentucky.

Page 91: *Comparing Old Living Things* by Jayme Asbell-Luckau.

Page 93: *King Solomon Writing Proverbs*, engraving by Gustave Doré, 1850.

Page 96: *The Miraculous Birth of Isaac* from freebibleimages.org.

Page 99: *Piece of Dead Sea Scrolls.* Courtesy of Wikimedia Commons; for more information, visit www.commons.wikimedia.org.

Page 100: *Ancient Scroll.* Courtesy of Wikimedia Commons; for more information, visit www.commons.wikimedia.org.

Page 103: *Cain and Abel* by Amalfi, c. 1084. Louvre, Paris.

Page 105: *Death of Abimelech* by Gustave Doré, 1866.

Page 106: Section from *Massacre of the Innocents* by Guido Reni, 1611. Pinacoteca Nazionale di Bologna, Bologna, Italy.

Page 106: *Jezebel* by Jayme Asbell-Luckau.

Page 108: *Herodias* by Bernardino Luini, 1527. Uffizi Gallery, Florence, Italy.

Page 109: *Jesus' Trial before Caiaphas*, from the woodcuts for the Picture Bible by Julius Schnorr von Carolsfeld, 1852–60.

Page 111: *King Noah* by Jayme-Asbell-Luckau.

Page 116: *The Kiss of Judas* by Alexandre Bida, from *Christ in Art or The Gospel Life of Jesus: With the Bida Illustrations*, Edward Eggleston (New York: Fords, Howard, & Hulbert, 1874).

Page 122: *Flight into Egypt* by Eugene Alexis Girardet, 1853–1907.

Page 122: *Nehemiah*, from freebibleimages.org.

Page 123: *19th Century Wood Cut of a Mormon Pioneer Wagon Train* from *Wife No. 19 or A Life in Bondage* by Ann-Eliza Young, 1875.

Page 125: *Paul's Journey to Rome.* Courtesy of Wikimedia Commons; for more information, visit www.commons.wikimedia.org.

Page 127: *Mormon Battalion Monument* by Edward J. Fraughton, in Presidio Park, San Diego, California. Permission via Creative Commons License; for more information, visit https://creativecommons.org/licenses/by-sa/3.0/deed.en.

Page 129: *Clipper Ship.* Courtesy of Wikimedia Commons; for more information, visit www.commons.wikimedia.org.

Page 130: *Jaredite Journey* by Jayme Asbell-Luckau.

Page 132: *Lehite Journey* by Jayme Asbell-Luckau.

Page 132: *Sailing Ship in Storm.* Courtesy of Wikimedia Commons; for more information, visit www.commons.wikimedia.org.

Page 133: *Gordon B. Hinckley,* modified by Mike Winder, based on the photograph by Boyd Ivey.

Page 138: *Abram's Journey from Ur to Canaan,* József Molnár, 1850. Hungarian National Gallery, Budapest.

Page 139: *Gold Coins.* Courtesy of Wikimedia Commons; for more information, visit www. commons.wikimedia.org.

Page 140: *The Visit of the Queen of Sheba to King Solomon* by Edward Poynter, 1890. Art Gallery of New South Wales, Sydney.

Page 141: *How King Solomon's Wealth Stacks Up* by Jayme Asbell-Luckau.

Page 142: *Feast of Ahasuerus* by Franz Hanfstaengl, 1836–52. Königlichen Galerie, Dresden, Germany.

Page 143: *Christ and the Rich Young Ruler* by Heinrich Hofmann, 1889. Riverside Church, New York.

Page 149: *Edward Hunter* by Charles Roscoe Savage, ca. 1873–1883. Harold B. Lee Library, Brigham Young University, Provo, Utah.

Page 150: *Brigham Young* by Charles William Carter, 1866. Harvard Art Museum/Fogg Museum, Cambridge, Massachusetts.

Page 153: *Artist's Rendering of a Colliding Wind Binary* by C. Reed, NASA.

Page 155: *The Kolob System* by Jayme Asbell-Luckau.

Page 156: *Archangel Sandalphon* by Steve Truett, freeware desktop wallpaper.

Page 157: Facsimile no. 2, Book of Abraham, Pearl of Great Price.

Page 157: *Gibbous Moon* by Opoterser. Permission via Creative Commons License; for more information, visit https://creativecommons.org/licenses/by-sa/3.0/deed.en.

Page 159: *Ancient Astronomer in Egypt* by Camille Flammarion, 1880. *Astronomie Populaire,* Paris.

Page 160: *God Creating Heaven and Earth* by Antonio Tempesta, 1555–1630. Florence, Italy.

Page 161: *Sunrise over Earth,* NASA.

Page 161: *Andromeda Galaxy,* NASA.

Page 162: *Africa from Space,* NASA.

Page 165: *Horsehead Nebulas,* NASA.

Page 171: *Quail.* Courtesy of Wikimedia Commons; for more information, visit www.commons.wikimedia.org.

Page 171: *Veal.* Courtesy of Wikimedia Commons; for more information, visit www.commons.wikimedia.org.

Page 172: *Beef Steak.* Courtesy of Wikimedia Commons; for more information, visit www. commons.wikimedia.org.

Page 173: *Loaves and Fishes* by Jayme Asbell-Luckau.

Page 175: *Basket of Figs.* Courtesy of Wikimedia Commons; for more information, visit www. commons.wikimedia.org.

Page 176: *Fruit and Cheese.* Courtesy of Wikimedia Commons; for more information, visit www. commons.wikimedia.org.

Page 177: *Broiled Tilapia.* Courtesy of Wikimedia Commons; for more information, visit www. commons.wikimedia.org.

Page 177: *Spies Returning Fruit from Promised Land,* from freebibleimages.org.

Page 178: *Fruit Bowl.* Courtesy of Wikimedia Commons; for more information, visit www. commons.wikimedia.org.

Page 181: *Captain America/Moroni,* a mashup by Mike Winder.

Page 182: *Samson* by Mike Winder.

Page 182: *Teancum* by Jayme Asbell-Luckau.

Page 184: *Michael and Angels Fight the Dragon* by Julius Schnorr von Carolsfeld, illustration for "Das Buch der Bucher in Bildern," Verlag von Georg Wigand, 1908. Liepzig, Germany.

Page 184: *David and Goliath,* from freebibleimages. org.

Page 186: *Nephi's Shock* by Mike Winder.

Page 187: *Samuel the Lamanite* by Mike Winder.

Page 188: *Daniel and Lions* by Jayme Asbell-Luckau.

Page 190: *The Story of Shadrach, Meshach, and Abednego* by Philip Galle, 1565. Los Angeles County Museum of Art.

Page 191: *Jonah's Whale Compared to Sperm Whales* by Jayme Asbell-Luckau.

Page 194: Modified by Mike Winder, based on art shared by http://jesus-christ.wikia.com.

# ABOUT *the* AUTHOR

Michael Kent Winder is the author of twelve published books, including the regional bestseller Presidents and Prophets. Mike is the CEO of Neptune Strategies, and as a former mayor of West Valley City, Utah, he remains active in community service. He holds an MBA and honors BA in history from the University of Utah and graduated from an executive program at Harvard University's Kennedy School of Government. Mike and his wife, Karyn, are the parents of two girls and two boys.